Does Anything Eat Shit?

AND 101 OTHER CRAP QUESTIONS AND ANSWERS

SARAH HERMAN

summersdale

DOES ANYTHING EAT SHIT?

Copyright © Summersdale Publishers Ltd, 2007

Reprinted 2007

Text by Sarah Herman

Illustrations by Harry Malt

Summersdale Publishers Ltd
46 West Street
Chichester
West Sussex
PO19 1RP
UK

www.summersdale.com

Printed and bound in Great Britain

ISBN: 1-84024-606-5
ISBN 13: 978-1-84024-606-3

For Lowri and Jameils (the Tripod) – because if it
didn't have three legs, it wouldn't stand up.

Acknowledgements

Big back-slapping thanks to…

Captain Lucy 'Pevs' York for her fine mind, fabulous editing skills and impressive right hook. You have made sense where there was none, guiding this shadowy vessel through the storm to a sandy beach, bottle of rum and a plate of homemade nachos. Aaarrrrr me hearties!

The Grand Page Master, Rob Smith, for hovering, consumption in the face of adversity and general design wizardry.

Director of many things, Jen Barclay, for knowing that laughter, cake and wine are very important.

And all the other fabulous folk at Summersdale HQ without whom I would be nothing but a short homeless person with no job and very messy hair.

Contents

Foreword

Living in modern times, as I do, there are plenty of reasons to be paranoid, and the fear of the unknown hangs over me like a pretty tall person leaning slightly to their right. With the collective brain of my fellow man in mind I have taken it upon myself to answer all the questions that few would even dare to ask and offer them to you in exchange for some money (unfortunately, even knowledge has a price).

Open your mind and prepare to be a vessel for my wisdom; in these pages you will find steaming piles of facts gained by hanging around in libraries trying to look studious, nuggets of truth just waiting to be plucked by your wandering hands and floating logs of genius ready to rescue you from the sea of ignorance.

This is a bible for all those people who feel lost and trapped in a world where there is too much certainty and not enough nonsense. I don't claim to have all the answers, but I hope you find some solace and the occasional titter in the ones that I have provided.

Plato once said: 'Science is nothing but perception.' And he was a wiser man than me.

Sarah Herman

FUNNY FOOD

Do Jelly babies have feelings?

The story of the jelly baby began in Victorian England, when village shop owners began looking around for new treats to make them rich. It was a Cornish woman who literally stumbled across a brand new chewy treat while out walking her dogs on the beach.

Thousands of jelly babies (or *Catostylus mosaicus miniacus*) had been caught up in a strong south Atlantic current, carried thousands of miles from the Liberian coastal city of Monrovia (their usual winter migratory spot) and washed up on the beach in Widemouth Bay. These tiny white members of the *Scyphozoan* class, who lay confused and cold on the sand, suddenly found themselves being devoured by two large Irish Setters. When the Cornish confectioner saw how popular these little human-shaped jellyfish were with her dogs she collected a sample and conducted a series of tortuous taste tests, injecting flavourings and dyes into the screaming little creatures whilst they were still alive.

Because of their small size it was too difficult and messy to kill them, so instead she opted for a tasteless wax-based coating that paralysed the bodies of the 'babies' and forced their insides to settle into a single soft jelly cell. Jelly Babies were an instant hit, with children up and down Britain merrily biting the heads and appendages off these defenceless little creatures. Concerned that demand would outweigh supply, she set up a fish farm and sent a few 'babies' out to sea in the hope that an SOS would be delivered to jelly baby colonies around the world. Sure enough, the following year, thousands more arrived and were caught in extravagant nets and delivered to her farm, where she was able to establish a breeding colony that has continued to supply sweet-toothed kiddies with their favourite sugary treats to this very day.

Although it is believed that the paralytic coating does prevent the babies from feeling any physical pain when chewed, they are very much alive and scared when you eat them.

What would be more likely to survive a nuclear explosion - cockroaches or pickled onions?

After the sacrifice of many cockroaches in the name of science, radiologists have discovered that the American variety of these hard-core bugs can withstand 67,500 rems of radiation (a rem is a unit of effective absorbed radiation in tissue), whereas German cockroaches can survive between 90,000 and 105,000 rems, probably due to a severe sunbathing regime which hardens them to the effects of radiation on their outer shells. When the bad guys do succeed in detonating a worldwide series of nuclear bombs to bring about the end of capitalism, and indeed themselves, if they manage to avoid the initial blasts, cockroaches will still be hanging around wiggling their pointless little antennae.

However, while we humans can be killed off by a pretty pathetic 800 rems, scientists in Scotland are working with chip shop owners to develop a new strain of pickling brine that enables fermented goods to remain impenetrable to thermonuclear radiation. By slowing down the cell reproduction process in onions (and possibly gherkins) and therefore reducing the window in which radiation can affect them, if sealed in a reinforced anti-hydrodynamic container these nutritious and popular snacks could not only survive the initial blast but would remain intact and edible for years afterwards.

While cockroaches have been known to survive without a head for up to a month, and without food for the same amount of time, unlike the trusty pickled onion, they will have to eat at some point. Although they will face tough competition from various other insect species who have also avoided fallout, it's likely their omnivorous nature and team-work mentality will work to their advantage. But provided the pickled onion containers are coated in a hydramethylnon gel, there's no way the cockroaches will consider them a viable food source. They will eventually die of starvation, but the pickled onions will remain. What a shame we won't be around to eat them.

Can beans really make you fart?

During World War Two, the RAF posed as Luftwaffe supply teams and dropped bogus supplies over the German trenches. Their intention was to weaken the German ground-level troops by causing serious ill-health. Amongst the lethal foods they deposited were Cherry Bakewells laced with solanine (a poison that affects the gastrointestinal system), gravy granules with ground up arsenic in them and baked beans (because they'd just been invented and the British soldiers were suspicious of them).

Surprisingly, it was the beans that had the most powerful effect. As the tins were unopened, the Germans rightly believed them to be poison free and hungrily ate the lot. The next day they had planned a surprise over-the-top attack on a weak spot in the British trenches. But as they approached they began farting left, right and centre. The situation was uncontrollable and the smell unbelievable, even over the stench of the trenches. Heralded by their involuntary battle cries, the Germans lost the element of surprise and the British soon forced them back behind enemy lines.

The British have been great fans of the flatulence-causing baked bean ever since. High in polysaccharides and oligosaccharides such as inulin, they actually increase the rapid evacuation of gas from the lower intestine (the amount you let rip) and the pungency of the air you expel. Other foods on the 'fart' list are lentils, cheap lager, onions, pepperoni pizza and cabbage, but none of these will produce an effect comparable in potency to that of the humble baked bean.

Why don't we drink breast milk into adulthood?

Breast milk used to be a luxury of the privileged aristocracy of the southern counties of England. Its high calcium and nutritional content made it one of the most sought after natural resources in Europe. Because it was considered a servant's work to feed children, wealthy mothers did not lactate and instead hired wet nurses to feed their babies and the lesser-known 'wet maids', who would express milk for the older members of the household. In fact, rich children were allowed to feed from their nurse until they were thirteen, when they would switch to bottles, a transition which was marked by a ceremony known as 'teet-aging' (this is where the word teenager derives from).

The British gentry's diet at the time consisted of fresh seasonal vegetables, meat and bread together with strong beer, wine and breast milk. Other products made from breast milk included breese (a creamy white cheese), brutter (similar to lard) and a cultured substance known as broghurt, which tasted like a sugary cottage cheese.

It was only with the advent of world exploration and overseas wars that wealthy men were forced (due to the absence of lactating women or any suitable refrigeration device) to drink the milk of cows, goats and kangaroos as an alternative. With the establishment of tea plantations and the growing obsession with the British 'cuppa', well-known faces amongst the gentry (known as the 'cowchops comrades') began to endorse the consumption of cow's milk as an alternative to breast milk. Farmers began to realise that there was a growing market for cow's milk and began mass production, providing a large consumer group with milk at an affordable price. More and more women left the lactating profession, enticed by the glamorous image of tall dark dairy farmers and milk-maid uniforms, and before long the breast milk industry became a thing of the past.

Nowadays there are occasional reports of celebrities drinking breast milk as part of a fad diet, but this is unlikely to catch on. However, some doctors still consider it to be a necessary component of a healthy diet and suggest that, if we happen to know a lactating mother, we drink at least one glass a week.

If you threw a crumpet off the top of the Empire State Building, would all the little holes help to slow its descent?

There are two basic types of parachutes – lift-producing chutes and pure drag chutes. A crumpet is essentially the latter in miniature form. Similar to a traditional hemisphere-shaped chute, the crumpet would generate a vertical drag force that goes against the direction of travel. Drag is produced when the air below a descending object is forced around its sides or (in the case of the crumpet) into small air pockets. The combination of flour and yeast make the skin of a crumpet very porous and as air became trapped in its many holes, the crumpet would slow down.

If wind conditions were favourable and the crumpet was dropped holey-side down, then the bumpy bottom and smooth top of this chute would ensure a gradual descent, with the textured surface creating sufficient friction to prevent the crumpet from speeding up. Most chutes are designed to carry something, but because of a crumpet's density it would not be able to support the weight of anything other that itself. To an onlooker it would appear that a small Frisbee or UFO was gliding gently to the earth.

Although crumpets tend to be very bland, if you are planning an experiment like this it is not advisable that you put butter or any other spread on the crumpet's surface. Not only will this increase the weight and decrease the number of holes available for air-trapping within the chute; the cool wind pressure at high altitude could also cause the spread to harden or even spill, making it an unpleasant cake-munching experience for the hungry receiver waiting at the bottom of the building.

Why do people throw tomatoes and eggs when surely coconuts would hurt more?

For centuries an unripe green coconut was the weapon of choice for local yobs and anyone attending a public humiliation down at the local market square. Before these tropical fruits arrived on our shores, if you happened to be walking past someone in the stocks you might throw a stone at them or tickle their feet, but you wouldn't dare waste food on them, even if it was rotten. But in 1777, during Captain Cook's third Pacific island voyage, a galley-hand discovered the coconut whilst out collecting supplies and, recognising its ridiculously hard qualities, saw a great business opportunity.

To distract other potential entrepreneurs from discovering his own intended use for the fruit, he wrapped the coconuts in banana leaves and used them as balls in the ship's Sunday five-a-side football tournaments (the first ever recorded example of the game being played). After arranging the importation of hundreds of coconuts he arrived back in England and set up a stall next to a popular stocks spot. At first business was slow, but when passers-by realised they could throw the coconuts repeatedly without them smashing and then take them home to ripen and eat afterwards, sales began to grow. Soon coconut stalls sprang up around the country and people were buying and throwing coconuts with such enthusiasm that the number of stock-related deaths rose by 40 per cent.

The government was happy; re-offending rates were down and public health was up because of the consumption of fresh fruit. But when British merchants in the colonies began to realise the money-making potential of the coconut they put up exportation costs and most stall-owners could no longer afford the rates. Diversification was in order and so stall owners set up a nationwide campaign to encourage people to throw at least five different types of rotten fruit and vegetables a week. Although people were reluctant to waste food, initiatives soon changed their minds. A popular offer was for every four tomatoes/eggs/cabbages that you bought to throw you got one free to eat. This in turn led to the introduction of stocks-smoothies, which you could either throw over the criminal or just sit back and slurp as you enjoyed watching that day's hanging.

Does anything eat shit?

While domesticated rabbits are quite happy to chow down on ceramic bowlfuls of carrot chunks and cereal, there's nothing their wild, burrowing relatives like to feast on more than a big pile of poo. The diet of these feral furry critters is limited to grass and, as they aren't equipped with a ruminant digestive system, they essentially have to eat their grass twice in order to extract its full nutritive value. What is less known about wild rabbits is that their coprophagous tendencies are not restricted to their own faecal matter.

A perfect sheep shit is considered a delicacy by these floppy-eared field folk, so when they locate a batch they immediately transport it to the nearest underground dining chamber and the Crap Crew (the bunny equivalent of the SAS) are sent out to retrieve suitable condiments (they favour Marmite) and cutlery to eat it with. When a particularly large shit is found, usually after a serious bout of bovine diarrhoea, entire warrens have been known to infiltrate motorway service stations to acquire large numbers of small plastic forks with which to devour nature's recent offerings.

The preferred type of shit and method of preparation tend to vary widely: some rabbits have been known to go to great lengths for a tiny amount of pigeon poop, whilst others are content to serve up a steaming plate of their own fresh droppings (or a dried version for breakfast which turns the milk chocolatey brown). This love of all things doo-deelicious led to the infamous 1998 Sewage Conflict where over 2,000 rabbits lost their lives defending a Devonshire sewage plant from closure – the stable food supply for seven warrens. Three council members were taken hostage for a month and forced to produce as much shit as they could, before the government conceded to the rabbits' terms and agreed to keep the plant open.

Why are fish eggs considered a delicacy?

Caviar began its edible life as a prop for a school prank and has ended up being one of the most sought after luxuries in the world. In the late 1800s, two young Iranian boys were fishing in the Caspian sea on a school trip when they both realised they were late for lunch. Knowing their head teacher was extremely strict, they gathered together a small pot of roe from the sturgeon they had caught and presented it to their teacher as a traditional local delicacy that they had been fetching from the neighbouring village. Not wanting to seem ignorant in front of his students, the teacher gorged himself on the fish eggs and, finding they were delicious, demanded the boys buy him large quantities to give as gifts to family and friends back home.

The local villagers caught on to the hysteria and began to fish for sturgeon in an effort to satisfy the appetites of visitors who were desperate to taste the delights of the region. The word began to spread westwards, but no matter which fish the Americans tried to extract roe from to produce a taste commensurate to that of the caviar they imported from Iran and Russia, they had no luck and were forced to pay the high prices the monopolised market demanded. Although highly sought after caviars such as Beluga, Ossetra and Sevruga cost as much as £30 per ounce, in their native countries they are still considered to be a local joke. Most people from caviar producing regions do not eat it when at home, but are often forced to partake in its consumption when abroad to keep up its appearance as a delicacy.

They also invented caviar etiquette to boost export sales of other products from their countries, stating that caviar should be served on crushed salted ice (preferably Caspian salt water), with a strong Russian vodka on a spoon made of mother of pearl from the Caspian coral reefs. If you must eat it with a cracker then, they say, it really should be a bretvich cracker (traditional Iranian breakfast bread).

Is it really Possible to eat all the Pies?

The pie has been around since about 2000 BC in ancient Egypt. At some point during the Greek settlements it was introduced to Roman culture, which is where the first known pie recipe (rye flour pastry with a goat's cheese and honey filling) originated. They first appeared in Britain in the twelfth century. At that time they were predominantly meat based and for a long time the crust was not eaten, but used merely as a preservative for the filling. But it wasn't until they jumped across the pond and were feasted on by the Americans that pie eating took off in a big way.

Competitive eating has always been a popular sport in the States. The televised coverage of Nathan's Hot Dog Eating Contest held at Coney Island on 4 July every year since 1916 and the formation of the IFOCE (International Federation of Competitive Eating) has led to the introduction of a number of large-scale world-renowned competitions of this sort. But none stick in the memory so well as the now infamous Palm Springs 1983 Pie Pig-Out. Competitors from as far afield as Japan, Vietnam, The Netherlands and (the former) Czechoslovakia gathered to spend 12 gruelling hours eating as many pork-based pies as they could.

A contest of this duration had never been attempted before, but organisers were keen to make the record books and the Pig-Out went ahead. Six hours into the competition, and after 17 extra deliveries of fresh pies, the food was fading fast and the 65 competitors were not slowing down. Pie manufacturers all over the country were contacted, but it was a Saturday afternoon so no one was producing pies. After a few final deliveries were flown in by private jet from Detroit and with two hours left on the clock, the organisers reluctantly announced the winner thus far and declared that the contestants had eaten 'all the pies in America'. Since then most pie-eating competitions are restricted to one hour, although fans of the sport say this doesn't effectively test a pie-eater's endurance ability.

No one has ever eaten all the pies in the entire world.

I married a really ugly man for his money. I know that certain foods are aphrodisiacs, but is there anything I can do to make sure he DOESN'T want to have sex with me?

There are plenty of things you can do to make sure your hunchback hubby won't want to do the horizontal tango with you once the lights go out. Obesity and anorexia are both known to reduce a person's libido considerably. This would involve subtly over- or under-feeding your partner until his body took over and a sex-shunning eating disorder kicked in. This could be quite tricky and although you want to discourage his sexual advances, you definitely don't want to be squashed on the rare occasions when you do have sex, or be made to feel like *you* need to drop a few dress sizes next to your size zero bed-buddy.

There is also the option of drugs. Testosterone is the hormone that controls his libido, and contraceptive pills, SSRIs and anti-psychotic medication have all been known to reduce this in males. However, there are known side effects, and the last thing you want at this stage is a boyfriend with webbed feet as well as his existing back hair.

The most effective method of turning your man off (besides forgetting to wax your moustache – although be warned, some boys find this irresistible) is stuffing his face with anaphrodisiacs. These foods have the opposite effect of aphrodisiacs and are proven to blunt the sexual appetite of even the most sexually active Tarzan. The berries, leaves and secreted oil from a chaste tree have been used throughout history and by various celibate religious groups to help men control their sexual appetite.

These, however, are not available at ASDA, and you will need to cook your man a dinner containing as much sedative potassium bromide as possible to keep sex off his mind. Also used to treat epilepsy in dogs and as a lust dampener for soldiers during World War Two, this chemical can be found in baked beans and most tinned preserved meats. I suggest preparing him a packed lunch so you don't have to eat it too, but a meal like this a few days a week will have him (voluntarily) sleeping on the sofa in no time.

If all else fails, make sure you're covered in his will and then push him off a cliff.

Why do broad beans taste better with your eyes closed?

It is true that when your eyes are closed your other senses, particularly smell, are heightened. Broad beans are rich in tyramine and vicine, two chemicals that produce satisfying, wholesome smells which the human body associates with nutritious food. But this only affects your initial reaction to a broad bean before you taste it. The broad bean has been in the human diet since 6000 BC and it is the pivotal role the bean has had in the social and political shaping of our world that has led to the misconception of its flavour, which in fact is no different whether your eyes are open or closed.

In ancient Greece and Rome, these beans were used as tools for voting. You cast your vote by the colour of the broad bean you selected and ate (white for yes, black for no), but many sceptics still relied on the gods to influence their vote and selected their bean blindfolded. This idea was later adopted by a number of religious groups who spread across the part of the world now known as Europe, claiming that it is only through suffering in the darkness that we can experience true joy and pleasure in life. As a symbolic act of their message they would invite followers to eat a broad bean with their eyes closed and declare how much better it tasted – a sign of their gods at work.

Although many of these traditions have been lost, in Italy broad beans are still known as *fave dei morti* or 'beans of the dead'. On St Joseph's Day it is considered disrespectful to those who have passed away to eat these beans with your eyes open and children are told that if they do they will 'taste the wrath of the devil'. American cowboys still test each other's nerve by selecting and eating a broad bean whilst blindfolded (uncooked bean pods are toxic). If you can choose a cooked bean without your sight you are considered to be a local hero. If not, you're probably dead.

If you bathed in wine, would you get drunk?

It has become a popular trend with the glitterati of la-la-land to take a soak in a tub of hot water topped up with a whole bottle of fine white wine. This is not just a hoax skin-firming fad invented by an off-licence that bought in too much stock. When activated by the high temperatures of the bath water, the ethanol content in the alcohol has an intensive dehydrating effect on the skin, blocking the pores and leaving your skin feeling 'as tight as a baby's ass'. Hollywood beauticians recommend using no more than one bottle per bath, as the gradual absorption of ethanol into the bloodstream can lead to drunkenness and drowsiness. They also advise against taking more than one wine-bath a week, as in the long term it can result in alcohol addiction.

These precautionary warnings are in place to dissuade anyone taking a bath consisting of an extremely high ratio of wine to water. If the wine is heated sufficiently, the impact on the central nervous system can be severe, especially if used as part of a daily skin regime. However, in Japan the sex industry has developed a treatment that maximises the effect of alcohol on the skin with a

Tokyo-based service offering male clients a hot wine-bath for the genitals. The thinness of the skin and the large number of blood vessels that exist in this area of the body mean that the intoxicating effects of the alcohol are instantaneous.

But be warned: despite the relaxing and skin-firming nature of wine-bathing, there are some undesirable side effects (in addition to the dangerous impact of alcohol poisoning). Some vineyards still use traditional methods of wine production, including ceremonial bare-foot stamping on the first harvested grapes and the use of wooden fermentation vats. The former is known to cause verrucas and fungal infections on the bather's body, and the latter can lead to woodworm in the bloodstream – infections and parasites that are ordinarily flushed out by the digestive system after drinking wine.

Why are chillies so hot?

Many cultures believe that chillies, most notably the strongest Bhut Jolokia variety, are the food of the devil, created to test religious leaders and remind humans of their insignificance and lowly status in the universe. Various rituals are performed in native chilli-growing areas to demonstrate the revered nature of this food and chilli-eating contests are held, with competitors reciting holy incantations and prayers to ward off bad spirits and help good win out over evil. Men who can consume vast amounts of the hottest local chillies in Cochabamba in Bolivia are considered wise and virtuous and are given pregnant goats at various festivals throughout the year as a mark of respect.

The physical feeling of 'spicy' that humans are familiar with is a chemical reaction that takes place in our own bodies when we consume foods such as chillies. They contain capsaicinoids which bind to the pain and heat receptors in our mouths, creating a burning sensation similar to how it would feel to French kiss a Valparaiso toad. These chilli molecules are low in electrons and are attracted to the electron-rich areas that exist on the heat-receptor surface. The more exposure you have to capsaicinoids (i.e. the more post-pub curries you consume), the more these receptors are broken down, allowing you to eat hotter chillies without feeling any effect.

Although the 'devil theory' has not been totally overlooked, it is much more likely that these foods – which other animals can eat without the same impact – have grown in areas of limited consumable plant-life to provide nutrients to creatures that live in areas where other foods are monopolised by humans. These receptor mutations exist to warn humans not to eat them so that some food will always be available for hungry lizards and tropical birds. Unfortunately, the invention of sour cream, guacamole and coconut-based curries have meant the majority of humans can withstand the most spicy chillies, forcing nature to produce ones that measure so high on the Scoville scale that the Pepper Institute at Ariba State University has been forced to cease taste experimentation.

Could instant noodles end world Poverty?

World poverty is an international problem which no one seems able to solve. It has long been recognised that handouts are not a lasting solution: the key is to facilitate self-sufficiency. In the past, attempts at encouraging self-sufficiency in poverty-stricken countries have been made through donations of farming equipment, wells and irrigation systems and by educating the people in land management, but still poverty exists.

The good news is that a more viable method of poverty elimination has now been identified: instant noodles. These dried, pre-cooked snacks, available for the bargain price of four pence per packet from most local supermarkets (cheaper if bought in bulk) come with a variety of nutritious flavourings. Their origin can be traced back to the Qing Dynasty in China, where noodles were stored for long periods of time by farmers who took them out into rural areas during the busy harvesting season. With the nearest Tesco Express hundreds of miles away, these light-weight consumables were a practical dietary supplement. But instant noodles as we know them today were a Japanese idea, voted for by their population as the most important invention of the last century; and it's not hard to see why.

A single serving is high in carbohydrates and fat; perfect for members of a hungry community. If factories were set up to produce the noodles for the local people in poverty-stricken regions, then not only would starvation be prevented but unemployment rates would drop. And they wouldn't even need access to a clean water supply to hydrate the noodles: the delightful sachet of powdered flavouring would mask the unsavoury taste of sewage and the chemical components would kill off bacteria.

Instant noodles were chosen in Thailand as a vehicle for dietary fortification by the Ministry of Public Health and they added minerals and vitamins to them, ensuring that these two-minute snacks could provide a tasty and balanced diet. One need only look at most university students who have been living off this diet in Britain for years to see that it is the foolproof answer Third World charities have been looking for.

Are there any super foods the government isn't telling us about?

The list of 12 phytonutrient rich or 'super' foods issued by government health advisers includes sweet potatoes, blueberries, deep fried chocolate bars and garlic. But do not be fooled. This is not a complete list, for there is one super food that has been 'accidentally' left out: spinach. The high levels of carotene, thiosulphonates and tannic acid present in the 12 known super foods can result in increased bone and muscle growth and better singing voices. But the international repercussions of public knowledge of the real power of spinach would be catastrophic.

Spinach is extremely rich in iron (one 60 gram serving contains nearly 20 times the normal level of iron in a green leafy vegetable). If you lived on a diet consisting of nothing but spinach for at least a year, you would start to develop EHS (Extreme *Homo sapiens*) strength levels and a muscle density to match. Interestingly, in 1890 a report leaked to an American newspaper by a Dr A. M. Rees (who was investigating the iron levels in a new German variety of spinach) proved this to be true. To prevent international panic and stock-buying of spinach, farms that grew the vegetable (predominantly in Texas and Arkansas, USA) were closed down.

In an effort to deflect public speculation about the real power of the green stuff, a comic strip called *Popeye* was created, which depicted a skinny man who developed Herculean powers after eating a can of spinach. The satirical nature of the cartoon was enough to convince the general public that Dr Rees's report was a journalistic hoax that had been in circulation for the best part of the twentieth century. But as time passed, and spinach and ricotta filo pastry parcels became a popular vegetarian dish of choice, it seems a more drastic approach was needed. In 2006 spinach coming from 21 US states was found to be infected with a strain of E. coli. This was followed by an FDA press release warning people against eating it. Since then nationwide spinach consumption and exportation to other countries has dropped by 80 per cent.

Is it Possible to bake blackbirds in a Pie as in the nursery rhyme?

Baking surprises into pies and pastries was fashionable in the 1700s and although 'Sing a Song of Sixpence' was in fact a recruitment ditty for the notorious pirate Captain Blackbeard, it became popular because of its resonance with contemporary food trends of the time. Cooking animals alive in this manner was not uncommon. A chef to the British monarchy who wrote a best-selling Victorian recipe book called *Life in a Pie* recommended only 'half slaughtering' your ingredients to 'lock in the freshness'.

Today's animal cruelty laws would prevent this method of cooking. But assuming no one was looking, the best way to control the movement of the birds and to ensure they remained in place during cooking would be to inject them with a small cocktail (2 ml per bird) of Diazepam and Ketamine which would relax their muscles and anesthetise them for four hours, enabling you to position the 24 birds into the pie. (You will need a deep, non-stick pie dish, diameter 80 cm.)

The relatively long cooking time on a low heat setting will prevent the chemicals in the birds' bodies from over-heating, which would cause the muscles to spasm and could affect the overall look of your shortcrust pastry. (For those using ready-made puff pastry, a slightly higher cooking temperature can be used.) On removing the pie from the oven and slicing for your guests, be careful not to cut the birds. Although they will be very much dead by this point, the air trapped in their lungs will be released when pressed gently by a fork to make your dinner whistle the song of a blackbird – the perfect entertainment for any dinner party!

NB: Blackbird pie is best served warm on a bed of seared asparagus tips, with wholegrain mustard mash and a dry Chardonnay.

Why are sprouts so small?

The Brussels sprout that we have traditionally come to hate – but always seem to be served at Christmas, nestling in a pool of gravy next to the roast parsnips and herby stuffing – is not supposed to be small at all. In fact, this leafy green member of the wild cabbage family, which was originally cultivated in Brussels, was a staple part of every family's diet during the sixteenth century due to its epic proportions and practical production methods.

Most households owned Brussels plants, which grow incredibly slowly as one long continuous stalk. Once it reaches optimum length, the plant produces over fifty buds along the length of the stalk, then automatically suspends growth in all but one bud, leaving the rest of the plant in a dormant 'coma-like' state. Then, one by one, it supplies each bud with sufficient water and nutrients to help it grow into a large, bulbous cabbage, not moving on to the next until the previous sprout has reached maximum growth. Thanks to the extensive root network and incredibly efficient nutrient and water absorption rate of the plant, this growth process would take a maximum of seven days per bud, guaranteeing a family on average one large cabbage per week.

In the Victorian era the British began to celebrate Christmas in style, with more and more dishes of imported meats and vegetables being displayed by the aristocracy as a sign of their wealth. Unaware of the sprout's growth patterns, British servants and cooks presented the buds to their masters as novelty 'mini-cabbages' – which went down a storm – thereby creating the famous Christmas food tradition we have today. Because boiling was an expensive and time-consuming method of preparation, the sprouts were instead fried and were rarely cooked in water. It is this over-boiling which releases sulphur compounds stored in the bud (intended as an initial nutrient supply to enable growth) and makes Brussels sprouts smell so bad.

What really happens to chewing gum when you swallow it?

The old wives' tale goes that if you swallow chewing gum it will take seven years for your body to fully digest it. In actual fact, chewing gum is never fully digested by the body at all. The gum base, made predominantly of rubber and petroleum polymers, is broken down by stomach enzymes into a thin, gluey substance that passes though the ileum (small bowel) and then, due to its high sugar content and water-like consistency, from the colon into the bloodstream. Once this gummy solution reaches the kidney, it is too bulky to be filtered out with urea and remains clinging to the red blood cells as they continue around the body.

This increase of 'rubber' in the bloodstream also means a gum swallower can easily withstand 800 volts of electricity being passed through their body, while a gum spitter can only endure 240. It has become tradition for death row prisoners in Nebraska to swallow vast amounts of chewing gum the week before they face the electric chair, in the hope that it will save them from their fate.

And almost all letters from supporters and fans include a packet or gum or a piece of car tyre as a well-wishing gift.

On the whole we're spitters not swallowers and will not consume enough gum in a lifetime to develop any serious side effects. In Mexico, where chewing gum was invented in the 1860s, people have been swallowing their gum for generations, undeterred by government health warnings and advertising campaigns. The glue-like consistency of most Mexican people's blood means there is little risk of haemorrhaging from an open wound, and the rubbery texture of their body tissue means they remain physically mobile much longer into old age. The resilience of the Mexican body is put through a series of tests every year at the Tampico Games where contestants throw their bodies at brick walls, run across beds of nails and bounce their children over nets in an elaborate 'human tennis' tournament.

What would be more palatable - your own sick or someone else's?

The taste of our own sick is not pleasant because of the acidic reflux from our stomach. It is the taste of our own bile that remains in our mouth after vomiting, together with some of the salt content we have lost. This delicate balance of salts, acids and enzymes makes up the taste of our sick and the taste of others'. Eating the sick of someone from your own genetic pool (such as a family member) is preferable because the basic chemical content will be the same – meaning you won't have a reaction to any foreign bodies – whilst the acidic taste will be different enough for you not to recognise it as sick.

Taste tests were carried out at the Kilbride Medical Centre in London with 'healthy sick' from a number of family and non-family members as well as some vomit from a number of healthy animals. Blindfolded participants were unable to stomach their own vomit, or that of humans not related to them, but found their close relations' sick edible. However, the most surprising result from the experiment was that dog sick was enjoyed by 82 per cent of the subjects, most of whom said they would eat it again and with one gentleman referring to it as 'not dissimilar from a mild watercress and leek soup'.

The practice of sick consumption is known as vomitophagia and is carried out in four known ethnic groups around the world. It is often ceremonial and has religious relevance, with individuals forcing themselves to be sick as a symbol of sacrifice to their gods. On one South Pacific island, there is an ancient tribe known as the Kungualla. After their annual harvest festival, known as 'Lulu', the head of each family must be sick after feasting on the foods that have grown successfully on the island. This sick is not seen as disgusting, but rather as food blessed by the land god and appreciated by the people. Each member of the community must then eat a mouthful of sick produced by another family, thus binding the community together through its harvest. Because of interbreeding in the small community, the vomit is more palatable.

How do they get the seeds out of grapes?

Not content with the wonders nature provides for us, we're forever trying to find a way to modify food to suit our needs. The very notion of a seedless grape was laughed at 50 years ago because it takes away the very essence of what allows that grape to procreate and therefore exist in the first place. But admittedly it's a real nuisance biting into a sweet, succulent fruit only to be met by a hard, bitter pip that's liable to get stuck in your teeth. So when someone came up with technology that could rid us of these nasty surprises for good, grape producers were eager to get their hands on it.

The grape-bug is a microscopic, remote-controlled robot that is powered by a tiny digital receiver. They are injected into the root of the grape vine and travel through the branches, along the stems and into the fruit, systematically destroying each seed (which is identified by its acidity level) with a laser beam before self-destructing after three days. Sometimes they will malfunction and you may find a couple of grapes amongst a 'seedless' bunch still have their seeds intact, or you will experience a small amount of indigestion after eating grapes (this is down to an un-destructed bug being broken down in your intestines) – but more often than not the grape-bug works as predicted and eliminates the existence of seeds, leaving your grapes pip-free and your chompers intact.

Grapes *sans* seeds are of a lower nutritional value than their seedy counterparts but are preferred by 78 per cent of grape-eaters worldwide. Most wine producers use seedy grapes because of the effect the extra acidity has on the fermentation process, but some new wines produced from seedless grapes have received a positive critical response and are said to be particularly 'minty' on the nose.

Cress seeds aside, what increases in nutritional value when left on a damp paper towel?

The majority of natural foods (vegetables, fruit, animal products) are at their highest nutritional value when first harvested or killed and leaving them on a damp paper towel at room temperature would result in a substantial and rapid loss of nutrients. However, this is not always the case with some manufactured or man-made food products.

Some brands of cheese and onion crisps contain high levels of kidney bean extract. When the crisps are dampened (in your mouth) the wholesome taste of the bean is activated to produce a full, satisfied feeling in the stomach after consumption. However, if the crisps were left on a damp paper towel in a warm room (or in your mouth for a long period of time) any seeds present in the kidney bean extract would begin to sprout. An entire packet of crisps creates some interesting results – as the crisps dampen, go mouldy and disintegrate, the bean shoots begin to form, leaving you with the base for a traditional South American bean chilli (far more nutritious than a packet of crisps).

Most carbonated soft drinks would also increase in nutritional value if poured onto a paper towel, though in this case it would not need to be damp to begin with. The paper towel would act as a filtration system: the harmful E-number additives would rest on the surface of the towel, whist the dissolved natural sugars (derived from any natural additives or flavourings e.g. orange) and water would pass through to the other side of the towel. You would need to find an effective way of collecting this purified liquid, which would be considerably healthier for you than what it came from. The taste would not be dissimilar to warm sugar water – the perfect accompaniment to a spicy bean chilli.

How many cooks spoil a broth?

To make a good broth you will need the bones of an animal, enough water to cover them, a touch of vinegar and optional assorted vegetable scraps. Put the bones in a pot, add the water, vinegar and veg, bring to a simmer and just sit back. No fancy chopping, delicate mixing of expensive ingredients or artistic presentation – this is caveman cooking, and it requires a caveman's sense of time. A spoiled broth is usually the result of meddling and impatience and the more cooks you have the more chance someone will crack under the pressure of a two day wait and force the remaining chefs to remove the pot from the heat prematurely. A shift system for the duration of cooking would help prevent such a disaster and no more than three cooks are required to strain, cool and divide up the broth into clearly labelled Tupperware containers. All cooks should wear name badges for instant identification and rubber gloves for health and safety reasons.

Of course, home cooking nowadays is much more multi-cultural than it was in the days of the cavemen. Things work slightly differently if you are planning on making a *dashi* (a simple soup stock, fundamental to Japanese cooking). Made from boiling shavings of *katseopushi* (goat's toe nails), *kombu* (edible kelp) and *keyurikatsee* (spicy lard), the cooking process involves just one person (traditionally the oldest female family member) and any deviation from this will result in a *bachi-dashi* which literally means 'cursed broth'. The Japanese believe that the balance of ingredients and delicate straining procedure must be the task of the individual who is considered to be the heart of the family because the combination of different textures and colours (in the way of meat and vegetables) can seriously affect the well-being of the family. Japanese restaurants do not serve *dashi* – to prepare this sacred family dish in a public eatery would not only curse the entire family for 15 generations, but anyone who set foot in the door or ordered a takeaway.

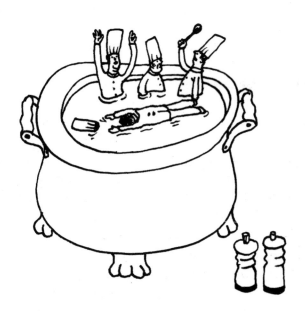

MY BODY AND ITS BITS

Is a small Penis really better than a big one?

The largest penis ever recorded, known as the 'Culligan Cock', was 29.86 inches long when erect. This is not normal and should not be seen as a point of comparison for the majority of men. That said, the average length of the male member is increasing, and at a faster rate than the average male height. A study published in the December 2000 *International Journal of Impotence* found that the average erect penis length was 5.35 inches long, but a 2007 online survey completed by 58,000 men put the current average at 6.4 inches. If this growth trend continues then by the end of the century the male sex organ could require its own carry-case for transportation.

But not all men end up with a penis of average size. In order to explain the seemingly random distribution of the micropenis (a penis whose erect length is less than 2.5 inches) it is necessary to look at historical representations. In ancient Greek art the romanticised image of man shows him with a relatively small, uncircumcised penis, as this was what was considered desirable at the time. Men and women alike preferred a less masculine image of man and those with large penises were ridiculed and usually forced to perform naked as gladiators, displaying their laughable forms to the public.

It wasn't until women started to develop a taste for seducing farm-hands and servants that they realised the merits of a well-endowed man. Since these days the large member has had a fair amount of bad press, being blamed for a number of high-profile incidents including the Gunpowder Plot, the Great Fire of London and the England Football Team's failure to win the World Cup post-1966. Although intercontinental and less incestuous breeding has made an 'average' size more common, there are an equal number of men with extremes of both sizes. It is society's modern attitudes towards masculinity and the capitalist notion that 'bigger is better' that have brought the big penis back into fashion, but this is only temporary, and if concrete evidence is brought forward to link big 'uns to the rise in British rail fares then it is more than likely that the micropenis will rule once again.

What does fear smell like?

When we experience fear, the brow and other parts of the body sweat dramatically to keep us cool as we flee the frightening situation. Unlike the perspiration produced during physical exercise, which is the excretion of toxins and liquid from the body through the skin, this is a light sweat that evaporates almost immediately after leaving the eccrine sweat glands. It is caused by the blood being moved quickly from one area of the body to another, transferring the necessary oxygen and proteins to the location that will require them in a fear-inducing situation – e.g. the legs, for running.

The sudden movement of these proteins often causes the body to speed up digestion and rapidly extract the vital chemicals from any matter being stored in the digestive tracts. This can produce an odorant known as gastro-methylphenol, which is excreted together with the water and sodium chloride onto the surface of the skin during 'fear-sweats'. It is this chemical that produces the individual smell of fear on a human. The odour will vary depending on the food present in the digestive chambers and can only be detected by animals with an abnormally keen sense of smell.

It is believed that the rare attacks on humans by great white sharks are caused by this odorant, which would commonly have a fish-related smell due to the diet available in most attack locations. An Australian couple left stranded off the coast of South Africa on a diving trip feared for their lives when they found themselves surrounded by three great whites. They tried to remain calm and after one hour of being nudged and circled by the sharks they were left alone. When they were found by a search team, local doctors questioned them about how they managed to survive. They weren't at all surprised to hear that the couple were vegetarians and had feasted on a breakfast of spinach, garlic and mushrooms that morning, which would have given a very distinctive odour to their fear.

'Great whites hate mushrooms,' one doctor is reported to have said. 'They wouldn't have eaten them if they'd been the last living thing in the ocean.'

Why don't humans have tails?

Despite external appearances, humans do in fact have tails. In the early stages of development, human embryos have protruding tails that measure one sixth of their entire body length, but as the embryo develops into a foetus that tail is withdrawn into the body. It is widely accepted that the tail bone (coccyx) is a vestigial structure. But this is only true in the minority of humans.

More often than not, the tail continues to develop inside a child until the age of eight or nine. This 'soft tail' contains no vertebrae, only blood vessels, muscles and nerves, and usually develops a pigment-free hair. The tail, due to growth space, is forced into a thin, coiled formation and remains trapped around the pelvis and lower spine until adolescent puberty. At the age of 13–16 in females and 15–18 in males, the brain releases a large quantity of neuropeptide hormones known as orexins which break down the structure (which has been known to reach 5 feet in length).

Complications during pregnancy – which doctors believe to be linked to heavy smoking, drinking, or a high gherkin intake – can cause the tail to remain outside the growing foetus. This is rare and the mother usually miscarries because the tail grows at a considerable rate and suffocates the baby. If it is spotted early enough, doctors can control the growth of the tail through hormone injections, and can remove it on the birth of the baby with a simple amputation procedure. There are reported cases of mothers who have declined the amputation. The longest human tail on record belonged to the French Indochinese son of such a mother. It measured 12 inches in length.

Where does the Tooth Fairy keep all the teeth?

As most people are aware, Tooth Fairy is the name given to the dental branch of Body Group – a multi-national organisation set up in the 1950s after the 1946 Stoke-on-Trent Treaty was signed to ensure that sustainable materials such as bone, hair and fingernails were effectively recycled by legal and safe methods. To encourage children not to simply throw their lost teeth away, the group devised a financial reward incentive, whereby parents paid a subscription to the service (a variety of packages were available to suit different families' means) and whenever their child lost a tooth a small representative from Tooth Fairy would arrive at the house late at night to leave whatever reward had been agreed, and to collect the tooth from the parents.

These teeth, along with waste hair from hairdressers and any other reusable body parts, would then be taken to the nearest Body Group recycling point and sorted for quality and future use. Teeth would be stored for six weeks in frozen chambers to remove all traces of plaque build-up and bacteria before being shipped to various clients, including jewellery makers, paint manufacturers and private collectors. The money received from the sale of teeth would then go back into public services such as NHS dentistry.

As Body Group became more transparent (following a number of undercover documentaries), it came to the public's attention that a lot of employees were setting up smuggling rings to move large numbers of teeth around the world. Parents became suspicious of Tooth Fairy representatives and found they were unable to cancel their expensive subscriptions. Fairygate proved to be a huge embarrassment for the government in the late 1980s and it was only after a televised public apology and a number of costly out-of-court settlements that things began to calm down.

Unfortunately, at a time when the environment could most benefit from this large-scale body-part recycling, the scheme is unavailable and parents prefer to keep the teeth for themselves, occasionally selling them on over the Internet. Needless to say, while the 'Tooth Fairy' name is still used throughout the world, without the much relied upon Body Group funds, NHS dentistry has become an under-funded and resource-starved public service.

Why do we have five toes?

Arguably, our precious pinkies are the redundant tools of ages past, when man was little more than a dribbling ape swinging through the trees with a firm-footed grasp. And now that tins have ring pulls, mobile phones are so small you lose them in your own hand and onions can be peeled, chopped, sliced and diced with one easy-to-use gadget, there is little need for the five phalanges of the human foot. Our fingers are quick and nimble and have taken over from their southern cousins.

In days gone by, *Homo erectus* was happy to still have the three large toes he inherited from his amphibian ancestors, webbed and pliable for efficient movement across forest canopies. They served little purpose for the plodding land dweller, however, and if it wasn't for the intervention of the arts then it is highly likely that toes would've gradually disappeared off the genetic map. For it was only when the earliest *Homo sapiens* decided to take up music that they began to serve a new purpose. Primitive instruments made up of rock and animal bone were created to produce battle noises and victory calls. As they needed their hands to perform the Mexican wave or make obscene gestures with giant foam fingers to neighbouring tribes, it is believed that early man used his feet to play music, developing the fourth and fifth toes as advantageous genetic mutations.

In fact, cavemen developed an early form of break-dancing whereby tribesmen would gather in large circular formations and compete in a movement contest, each taking a turn in the centre of the circle to challenge the leader's skills of agility and speed. The more toes you had, the more balanced and flexibile your body was, and the higher up the chain of command you fell. It is believed that the number of toes would have continued to rise to six or seven, had it not been for the invention of the shoe, which forced the toes to shrink back to mere stumps at the end of the human foot. In some remote cultures, having six toes is not uncommon.

If Grumpy from the Seven Dwarfs faced a hungry gorilla in a cage fight, is there any way he could win?

In normal circumstances it is unlikely that Grumpy, or indeed any of the Seven Dwarfs, could defeat a gorilla in a fight. However, if Grumpy were to take an intensive course of steroids in the time leading up to the fight then he would have a good chance of beating his hairy opponent. Assuming this is the case, the following is a prediction of how the fight would play out.

Grumpy's muscles will swell to three times their usual size and strength and although this could make him a little off balance at first, it will make him more than a match for the tough upper body of an adult gorilla. Drugged up on steroids, Grumpy will be extremely angry and pumped up for a fight, while the gorilla is going to be more interested in tracking down some food, scouring the audience on the outside of the cage for a few hotdogs and a super-sized coke. But when he spots the cellophane-wrapped banana sandwich tucked neatly inside Grumpy's coat pocket, he's going to use whatever's available to get hold of that snack.

If the 'no rules' rule of cage fighting is in place, Grumpy will be using whatever tools he has close to hand – his belt, a pick-axe, a miniature shovel and a bucket full of semi-precious stones if he's just been down the mine, whilst the gorilla will use anything it can get its hands on, be it steel chairs, empty rubbish bins or road signs.

A violent and exciting battle will ensue, and for a while it will look like the gorilla is winning, as he desperately lunges for the sandwich and refuses to back down. That is, of course, until Grumpy gets hold of one of the sponsor-supplied baseball bats covered in barbed wire. His steroid-pumped adrenaline will soar and spurred on by Snow White and the other Dwarfs cheering from the sidelines he'll beat the gorilla into a state of surrender, promising him a bite of a rather suspicious looking apple if he concedes.

Before silicone implants, how did girls ensure they had the biggest boobs?

For a long time, breasts have been big business. Even as far back as the twelfth century, when the very first strip club opened its doors, women have found ways to increase their chest size to please the lustful eyes of men. A popular method used throughout this period was a device known as the 'inflator'. The nipple would be removed with a scalpel and then the inflator would be attached to the hole, allowing heated air to be manually pumped into the chest. Thousands of women went under the pump to achieve the desired results. Most strip clubs had a duty surgeon present as in some cases the reattached nipples came loose during particularly athletic pole-dancing routines.

Despite the success of this method, scars were obvious and doctors continued to search for less obtrusive methods. In 1889 one doctor perfected the technique of injecting melted paraffin wax into his patients' breasts. The wax would mould itself to the natural shape of the breasts and then set hard at room temperature, creating a perfectly formed if somewhat immobile and potentially flammable bosom.

In the first part of the twentieth century the vaudeville and stripping industry boomed, with hundreds of girls auditioning for topless acts in London's West End and on Broadway as part of the war effort during the 1940s. And it was during this period that the Boob Race really took off. Over the years breasts were stuffed with light bulbs, ox-cartilage, sheep's wool, kryptonite, sponge and polystyrene balls. Many girls performed operations on each other because the cost of surgery was too high, leading to a number of high-profile fatalities.

The 1950s and 1960s saw the introduction of silicone injections which left over 50,000 women with deformed breasts and various serious health complications (the most dangerous method to date). Although relatively safe silicone implants are now available and breast enlargements are common place, fashion experts predict a fall in the market for big boobs and a rise in the popularity of the flat chest.

What makes knees knobbly?

We are born without knee caps and some of the essential ligaments that help the knee to function, and they do not begin to appear until two to six years of age. The human knee supports nearly the entire weight of the body and its effective development is paramount to our ability to walk and run. It is more common for the articular cartilages (at the front) and the menisci (at the side) to grow at the same rate, but in a minority of people this does not happen and the menisci grow faster, forcing the kneecap to mould itself around the bulging cartilage. This produces a knobbly appearance to the knee.

For people that have an average or low BMI, having 'knobbly knees' means their legs can easily support their body weight and their muscles are strengthened considerably more than someone with regular knees. They therefore make good athletes, especially long-distance runners, gymnasts and footballers and, depending on other medical conditions, can remain extremely mobile in later life.

Although it is less common in western culture, in some parts of the world there are a high number of genuphobes (people with a 'persistent, abnormal and unwarranted fear of knees'). This phobia causes breathlessness, excessive sweating and anxiety attacks. Knobbly knees are known to cause the most distress to sufferers. One Polish woman forced her husband and three children to have knee reduction surgery because she felt nauseous every time she looked at them.

Do moles contain wisdom?

There are two types of moles: congenital (those we have from birth) and acquired. The former are minor malformations caused during foetal development and are usually identified as small pigmented growths on the skin. These moles do not contain wisdom but have been attributed with various functions by individuals who, after having moles removed, have noticed a severe loss of sex drive, hair or ability to communicate with their teenage children. A Portuguese school caretaker once featured in a national newspaper for claiming that his mole was the door to a mystical land where the rivers were filled with gold – he charged students five euros to take a look.

Acquired moles are completely different. Some people will not develop any new moles throughout their life while others will notice new ones appear as they get older, even into old age. When new information is absorbed by the brain the cells are reordered and relocated to appropriate storage positions in the cerebrospinal fluid, depending on the type of information. This is known as neuronal migration. When the brain is overloaded with complex information, for example, during an algebra class or an episode of *Coronation Street*, the brain produces more cerebrospinal fluid than normal and the overspill will find its way down the spine and deposit the new cells into the blood vessels that supply the skin.

Over a period of time of consistent depositing an apparent mole will form on the skin; the dark colour is a result of the darker colouration of brain cells in relation to skin cells. A 1998 study by Fielding and Perrin revealed that of a sample of 300 Mensa International volunteers, 90 per cent had a lower IQ by ten points after the removal of three acquired moles.

Why does it hurt when a woman gives birth?

Aside from the obvious fact – that the stretching of the vaginal wall as a woman tries to push out a baby with a head the size of a small melon causes a certain amount of tearing and pain – there are much more important biological reasons for the agony a woman apparently experiences whilst in labour. It is very difficult for scientists to measure pain because people's thresholds vary, and when they are in pain they are not mentally sound enough to accurately define their own pain levels. What we do know through experiments performed on female dogs and horses whilst in labour is that their reaction to temperature and sensation is heightened. If you were to pat a dog on the head at any other time they would not even flinch, but when a dog is in labour being patted on the head is noticeably more distressing for them.

Similar experiments have been conducted on consenting women (although these are frowned upon, as any undue stress caused to a mother during labour could cause serious complications). If women's pain receptors are inflamed during childbirth then we can assume that they do not actually experience much more physical discomfort than a hung-over man might feel in a rugby scrum. However, their brain registers a much higher level of pain and therefore produces an exaggerated reaction – this explains the profuse sweating and screaming that occurs.

The biological reasoning behind this has been debated, but it is likely threefold. Firstly, the male of the species is less likely to help the female if she appears to be 'coping with it', so the screaming and visual agony she goes through encourages the male to be protective and to help where he can. Secondly, the mother, father and child are at their most vulnerable during childbirth and the screams of our female ancestors would have scared off any dangerous animals or enemies as it would sound like an attack was taking place. The third reason is thought to be that on hearing its mother's cries, the baby's instinctive response is to follow suit, thereby clearing its airway and kick-starting its lungs. In the modern world drugs are available to numb the pain, but women still scream, as this is what they have done for centuries and this is how nature intended it.

Wouldn't it be more useful if our arms were longer?

Our arms grow in proportion to our bodies. It is only rarely that a person will have particularly short arms or exceedingly long ones. The notion of the usefulness of really long arms to modern man is debatable. Whilst it would be nice to be able to poke someone in the post office queue when you're standing five metres away or reach for a cold beer in the fridge without moving off the sofa, the practicalities of Mr Tickle arms are seriously lacking.

Some teenagers are lucky enough to try this experience out. A small number of boys and girls don't produce enough growth regulator hormones during puberty. This results in a condition called hypophalimbism, where a taller adult height is reached by extra growth of the limbs. While the torso and pelvis remain of a standard size, the rest of the child grows at an alarmingly fast rate. These individuals, if diagnosed soon enough, can be given hormonal drugs to halt the process, but if the growth reaches a highly developed stage without treatment then the child has to wait a few years for the rest of their body to catch up.

One boy from a turkey farm in South Dakota was left in this state, and when his muscles grew strong enough to support the extra weight of his arms he was able to reach things he couldn't reach before and carry four turkeys instead of two. He said that having long arms was good for scratching your back, but other than that they just got in the way.

If you would like to make your arms longer you could try stretching for long periods of time, or there is a medical procedure which involves breaking the bone of the arm at various stages, moving it millimetres apart at a time and forcing the body to produce new bone to fill in the gap. This procedure is popular with dairy farmers, mechanics and tree-huggers.

Why does my nose bleed when I fly in economy class?

If you frequently experience nosebleeds when flying economy class, it's possible that you have Coach-bleed Syndrome (CBS), which affects about one in every 1,000 passengers. Cabin crew members for all airlines are given medical emergency training and are taught how to deal with the risks and problems that arise when a CBS sufferer has a serious episode. CBS is an autosomal dominant trait passed along genetically from father to child. The gene causes the growth of an inner layer of nasal tissue which is fed through a vast network of capillaries. When the sufferer is at low altitude the blood pressure within this complex network is at a normal rate, allowing the blood to move freely throughout the nose tissue – but when high altitudes are reached in a plane the sufferer is so sensitive to even the smallest changes in cabin pressure that the tissue expands, causing friction and then rupturing of the blood vessels.

CBS bleeds can be volcanic in nature, with blood being projected up to five metres from the nose and bleeds lasting for a number of hours. The real risk involved is when the burst capillaries are not removed from the nose with the use of a nasal-suction cone. If this does not take place then the bleed moves into stage two, known as 'brain-bleed', where the leaking capillaries feed off the brain's blood supply in order to function – there has only been one case of this occurring in the last twenty years when no nasal-suction cones were available because a member of cabin crew 'forgot to pack them'.

Interestingly, with an official doctor's certificate testifying that you suffer with CBS, you are entitled to sit in business or first class at no extra cost; airlines always reserve four seats in the business class for first-time flyers who are in economy and experience their first episode on the flight. This is because the window thickness in the front of the plane is greater, which means the cabin pressure is less and the tissue swelling considerably reduced. The complimentary alcohol also helps to increase the blood supply to the brain after a substantial nosebleed.

Is it possible to alter the colour of my urine?

There are a variety of ways you can dramatically change the colour of your urine. The yellow colour most of us are familiar with comes from the bile which is present in urine; the greater the ratio of excess water to bile, the paler your urine should be. If you have jaundice then your urine will be a dark orange to brown colour and blood in the urine (a sign of serious kidney problems) will, unsurprisingly, turn it red. Black urine (experienced by the majority of Caribbean pirates) is either a sign of a melanoma or a result of drinking copious amounts of dark rum whilst chewing liquorice root.

But without creating serious health risks to your body the most effective way to change the colour of your pee is through the consumption of various foodstuffs. Digesting lots of asparagus (green), beetroot (red) or blackcurrant cordial concentrate (purple) can have an obvious and short-lasting effect, whereas methylene blue (found in a number of popular alcopops) if consumed on a regular basis will not only stain the urine blue, but will also affect the colour of the oesophagus and stomach lining.

Pee paraders should be warned, however; lots of foreign countries have banned the public display (including in public toilets) of artificially pigmented urine on the grounds of health and safety. The legislation was pioneered in regions of southern Spain, Italy and Bulgaria after members of a bohemian cult left bottles of blue, red and coffee-coloured urine on the street (which were later drunk by some dogs, children and homeless people). It is believed the law could be introduced in the UK in the next few years.

Why do some people get goosebumps when they're stressed?

Breaking out in goosebumps when under stress appears to be a vestigial reflex in humans, remaining from when our evolutionary ancestors would raise their body hair to make them appear larger and more threatening to predators. Paradoxically, it is those people who have the least body hair who are most prone to experiencing goosebumps, and this is down to some sneaky medieval medicine.

In thirteenth-century Staffordshire it was difficult to make a respectable living as a physician unless you could provide a service that other local doctors could not. Joseph Branston was an up and coming GP looking to earn himself a fast buck and tapped into the female obsession with big lips that was sweeping the nation. He provided a service known as 'pouting', whereby he leeched blood from a family of chimpanzees that had been imported from central Africa and injected the blood into various cut points in the patient's arms, legs and face. He claimed that the increase in chimpanzee blood in the body would increase the levels of black bile (the humour supposedly responsible for producing fatty deposits in the lips and cheeks).

 His claims proved false but it wasn't until a few months after having the surgery that his patients began to notice something was wrong. There were two main reactions to the chimp blood; hair growth (in darker skinned/haired patients) and goosebumps in times of stress (in fairer women). The appearance of this reaction in the patients' subsequent children proved that the dominant chimpanzee DNA had integrated itself into the human genome, the results of which still exist today. After being found responsible for causing severe facial hair-growth on a visiting foreign princess, Branston was burnt at the stake for crimes against women and gross cosmetic misconduct.

Is there any way a smile could light up a room?

Obtaining the perfect 'Hollywood smile' has become an obsession of the Western world. Although it is natural for teeth to darken as we age, due to changes in the mineral structure of the tooth and the enamel becoming less porous, having white teeth is considered a sign of youth and beauty. There are various treatments available to make sure your teeth are the whitest on the red carpet. The most common method is to visit a cosmetic dentist and have each tooth treated with carbamide peroxide. This bleaching agent penetrates the crystalline structure of the enamel and bleaches both the enamel and the underlying dentine layer. The dentist will ensure the level of brightness is not unnatural looking.

There are home methods available for those who cannot afford this treatment which can, if used incorrectly, result in a much brighter colour, developing in luminosity for four to six hours after application. This procedure is repeated for a few hours a day over a two week period and, although this is a safer process and presents fewer risks to the soft mouth tissues, it can leave teeth looking unnaturally white. If under direct sunlight, the visual effect can be quite startling.

Without the aid of UV lights, teeth treated in this way could not, independently, generate light. However, in 2004 an American company called All Bright Products inc. managed to license an over-the-counter treatment that included phosphorescent powder, thus enabling people's teeth to glow in the dark. It was not until six months later, when the US Drug and Chemical Association realised that excessive use of this bleaching agent caused serious problems to the liver and kidneys, that the product was terminated. The company went under, but the product can still be bought illegally on the Internet, under the name of Glowteeth Cream.

How funny is my funny bone?

The exposed part of the ulnar nerve that runs from the shoulder to the hand (known as the 'giggle' nerve) is almost entirely responsible for your sense of humour. Although popular comedians don't like to admit it, their quick wit, genius one-liners and stand-up antics should not be credited to talent, skill and fine-tuned practice but to the size of their medial epicondyle or funny bone – the bump on the inner elbow that the ulnar nerve passes over. The larger your bump, the more exposed the nerve is and the sharper your humour receptors are.

To test the various theories that surround the funny bone's comedy credentials, a team of researchers travelled to a number of seaside towns around the UK on the Tall and Short All Star Comedy Tour 2006 measuring the size of each comedian's funny bone and comparing it to the 'laugh level' they measured on their gigglometer. Unfortunately, as the tour progressed it became apparent that most of the comedians had relatively small funny bones so there was no point of contrast, but it was recorded that none of the acts received a level of laughter substantial enough to register on the scale.

If your funny bone is small, chances are you're not very funny at all, and no amount of Peter Kay DVDs is going to change that. There are no funny bone enhancers available on the Western market and it's advisable to be suspicious of any you can buy over the Internet from South East Asia. Funny bone receptors only pick up on what's around them, so unless you've travelled extensively your sense of humour will be culture specific and a 'funny bone erector' from Singapore could make you seem even less funny to a British audience. If your bone is big, then you are one of the lucky ones and a career in open mic nights, politics or reality TV beckons.

Be sure to take care of your funny bone – cubital tunnel syndrome (when the nerve is obstructed and compressed, causing a 'pins and needles' sensation) can lead to severe damage and in some cases a complete loss of sense of humour. A large number of traffic wardens and bus drivers are thought to suffer from this condition.

I can't afford a designer baby - how can I ensure my child is good-looking?

Forget what you've heard about genetics, survival of the fittest and Koinophilia: having a good-looking child is within your control no matter how disadvantageous your own aesthetic circumstances. By following some simple rules you could be the proud parent of the next hot thing to end up posing naked for a classy men's (or women's) weekly.

It all starts before conception. The eggs of a human female all contain attractive genes – it is the sperm that have the potential to screw up the looks of any future children. To prevent the father from 'exsperminating' the chance of your little 'un making it in the world of beauty pageantry, he should spend at least 30 minutes every day doing lunges. (The gravitational swing on the testicles shakes up the sperm, catapulting the stronger, healthier and more attractive swimmers into poll-position.)

During the pregnancy, try to surround yourself with as many beautiful people as possible. The pheromones they give off will penetrate your skin and obstruct the production of U91Y cells in the embryo which develop into unattractive qualities such as hairy backs, bad skin and excessive sweating. If you don't know any beautiful people, holding copies of *Heat* magazine up to your stomach or sitting close to the TV during an episode of *Hollyoaks* could also be beneficial, depending on the thickness of the uterus wall and whether you have a high definition TV.

If either of the parents has any unattractive features it is recommended that you disguise these during the birth and for the first week of the child's life. This is when babies are most susceptible to VU rays (Very Ugly) that are emitted from the skin surrounding physical abnormalities, fatty areas and crooked teeth. These rays can seriously inhibit the beauty of your child and will have a dramatic effect on his or her future appearance. If either you or your partner's ugliness is severe, it's advisable that you have no contact with the child during this period and hire professional models to provide round-the-clock childcare. It'll be a worthwhile investment when you're watching your grown-up child prancing around in their underwear in the *Big Brother* house.

Could I chew my way out of a cardboard box?

Although this would be a lengthy and health-damaging activity, it is something that you could achieve. Your success would be measured in terms of the amount of time it took you to complete the task. In the absence of any other foods or drink, this could be quite challenging. If you did have access to sufficient food and water during the process and after a month you still hadn't eaten your way out of the box you would be officially diagnosed with the eating disorder known as Pica – the excessive consumption of non-nutritive substances including wood-based products. Pica sufferers usually eat a lot of pencils, cigarette butts and park benches. It is most common in children with developmental disabilities and pregnant women.

Apart from the possibilities of poisoning from any coating, paint or printing on your box of choice, you could receive splinters and paper cuts in your mouth and oesophagus and would be at great risk of sustaining a gastro-intestinal puncture (a tear in the stomach wall).

The process of eating the cardboard would be extremely difficult, especially without water or chocolate spread, but actually biting a hole from inside the box would probably cause you the most problems. Without a sharp implement or small existing hole, your incisors wouldn't be able to gain any purchase on the cardboard and eventually you would probably have to resort to opening the box with your arms to get out.

There is one recorded case of a man in America who ate his way out of a cardboard box that his friends had trapped him inside as part of a stag party prank. He was sent for a psychiatric consultation but also required surgery to remove a huge obstruction from his bowels. Since recovering in a psychiatric home in West Virginia he has developed a taste for various stationery and furniture. Doctors say his personality's become very 'wooden' and it could be a while before he starts trying to eat food again, as opposed to the packaging it comes in.

They recently discovered the 'fat gene' - are there any others we should know about?

A recent article in the *British Journal of Genetic Science* revealed that scientists are now rapidly breaking down the human genome and identifying more and more individual attribute genes as they do so. Among the genes to be identified so far, after the widely reported FTO (fat gene), are HB (heavy-breathing) and HB2 (hairy back). With the introduction of ID cards and retinal scanners, it's only a matter of time before the DNA Bubble – a small handheld device that allows authority figures to check your DNA for particular qualities – becomes commonplace in our day to day lives. This will mean that those who scan positive for HB will be turned away from cinemas, HB2 carriers will be shunned from public swimming pools and future political leaders will be scanned for GI (the general incompetence gene) before going to the ballot boxes.

As with everything, the Japanese are well ahead of the rest of the world, having already devised a way of turning these scientific discoveries into a commercial opportunity. A Tokyo-based company known as Gene Inc has recently opened a flagship Gene Store which they are looking to develop into a nationwide consumer chain. The store provides customers with a choice of 'gene chew' sweets that contain a small amount of a specific gene which is then absorbed by the bloodstream, providing the customer with up to three hours' experience of that particular quality. So far there are only a few options, and they are all non-physical. The most popular chew is known as 'Hot-stuff' which is derived from the 'confidence' gene. Others include – 'Giggles' (humour gene), 'Olympian' (competitive gene) and 'Petrol' (a banana milkshake flavoured sweet with a touch of the good-driver gene). Gene Inc eventually hope to open Gene Stores and Gene Bars around the world to cater to our growing curiosity.

Although UK scientists are well aware of these breakthroughs, a few years ago the Gene Control Act was passed in this country to prevent private business from capitalising on this technology, for fear it would result in anarchic behaviour. It was not widely reported (press attention was focused on the fox-hunting ban at the time) and it is only now that other countries are starting to embrace the gene market that the law is being reconsidered. This has led to recent sensationalised news stories about genetically engineered tanned children, goldfish gene injections to increase the size of your pout and 'the horn' – a pill which contains a cocktail of rabbit, horse and dog DNA to make the user 'like an animal' in the bedroom.

Why do our ears go red when someone is talking about us?

When you are a child, your own name is a sound that you become familiar with very early on. Even if you are not aware it is your name being said, you learn that if you respond to it by smiling, laughing, or even looking at the speaker directly, then a positive reaction will follow, including rewards. During the early stages of muscle development, it is not always possible for a baby to smile or control the movement of their body parts, so rather than produce an oral or physical movement response, the default reaction of the cerebral cortex (the part of the brain that interprets sound) is to increase the blood flow to the adipose tissue of the cheeks, ear lobes and the perichondrium membrane of the auricles (left ear for high frequencies and right for lower frequencies). This gives the face and ears a red appearance, so the baby's parents will know that their child has heard them.

As we get older and are able to produce a variety of responses to the sound of our name, this 'blood-surging' recedes. The highly sensitive hair cells in the ear can pick up on the familiar sound of our name if it is spoken within a 40 metre radius of us. If someone we're interacting with says our name, or someone calls to us from a distance, our reaction is either oral (to make conversation) or physical (to look and wave), but if someone says our name to another person within 'earshot' of us then there is often no response, and the blood-surging default is activated.

The distribution of blood to either the right or left ear has helped to create the saying: 'Left for love, right for spite.' This is actually fairly accurate because if someone is using your name in a positive way, they're more likely to be talking in a higher frequency, meaning that your left ear would become illuminated.

I keep dreaming that I have a moustache, but I'm a girl: what does this mean?

Many 'dream experts' and books that claim to interpret the meaning of dreams will tell you that these subconscious thoughts are an indication that you take a very masculine role in your personal and work relationships and that you are anxious about not being feminine enough. Although this anxiety may be a factor in your life, it is not the real reason you have these dreams.

After puberty a few people experience unexpected hair growth. Although this is more common in old age, occasionally it occurs before then. This hair growth usually takes place during sleep and triggers an SEM (subliminal electro-murmur); an electric impulse that causes the brain to create images of future hair growth. Sometimes these images are confused and the dreamer will have visions of tooth extraction or small winged ponies.

In her recent thesis, *My Moustache and Me*, leading authority on the study of SEMs Dr F. Woolerton says: 'These murmurs are a useful indication to women that their bodies are changing, and nature's way of telling you to book yourself in for an upper lip wax.' Woolerton goes on to say that if a woman dreams that she has a goatee it usually means her nipples are sprouting new hairs, although there is only a small body of evidence to support this claim.

There's no real need to panic though. A moustache on a woman is a sign of sexual stamina and power and could be the key to getting that big promotion or convincing your boyfriend (if he's still with you) to do a bit of housework. There are plenty of great facial hair accessories on the market and it's a great excuse to get another bag; after all, you'll need somewhere to keep your moustache comb.

Could I make candles out of my ear wax?

Most people are unaware that there are three genetically determined types of human ear wax: wet wax (the dominant type), found in the majority of Africans and most Caucasians; dry wax, found mostly in the ears of Asians and Native Americans; and grain wax (the recessive type), which is most common among North Europeans, especially Finnish, Norwegian and Swedish people. All three are made up of cerumen, a mixture of viscous secretions, namely squalene, lanosterol and cholesterol, but the genetic coding determines the colour, consistency and waxy quality of each type.

Ear candling is a traditional method of removing excessive ear wax which was practised widely in Northern Europe and Russia until the introduction of syringing in the late twentieth century. It involves placing a hollow candle in the ear canal and lighting it. The rising hot air draws out toxins and the melting ear wax drips down and collects in the hollow candle. The coarse consistency of grain wax is the only one of the three to harden into a solid form not dissimilar to beeswax, and can be moulded into a useable candle form.

One Finnish candle maker, now serving a prison sentence for a series of fraud charges, posed as a health specialist and set up a therapy centre for blocked ears. Using electric heating devices he began extracting large amounts of free wax from people to use for his candle business, whilst charging them for their 'donations'. Most British ears are unable to produce candle wax, but this hasn't stopped a number of high-profile artists from trying to create sculptures out of the sticky stuff in their ears.

MAN-MADE
MATTER

I'm planning on building a gingerbread house to get on Grand Designs - any advice?

Gingerbread biscuit is not an ideal building material for a habitual structure, but that doesn't mean it can't be used to create the family home you've always dreamed of. Of all the biscuit varieties, these spicy treats are the most capable of withstanding high cooking temperatures and long cooling periods, making them adaptable to a number of essential building requirements. The combination of treacle, corn flour and a touch of fine-lime cement should ensure a hard, strong substance suitable for walking on if set thickly over the foundations. Please consult Lady Fleming's original dough recipe for the most effective gingerbread floor, walls and roof.

Depending on the climate where you're building your house, you may experience some structural shifting due to heating and cooling once the structure has been built, but this is no different to the majority of wood-based houses. To ensure a water-tight finish you may have to add a polyresterlaine lining to the outer walls and roof, but make no mistake; constant maintenance will be needed to address soggy patches of biscuit. Please keep in mind that although buttercream would make the tastiest glue to stick your house together, it will definitely not be the most durable and, if you must use it, combine it with a raspberry jam (bought from a local farmers' market) for maximum aesthetic appeal.

It's fashionable nowadays to produce an eco-friendly home that has minimal impact on the surrounding environment. Stored in an airtight container at room temperature, gingerbread can have a shelf life of a few months, but under temperamental conditions the house should stand for at least two weeks. If built in the countryside it will provide a veritable feast for the local wildlife and small children, without leaving behind waste products. To increase your chances of getting your house on the show try adding in a few solar panels and a stylish wind turbine; however, under-floor heating is not recommended.

If you lay on 20 mattresses on top of a pea, would you be able to feel the pea?

Ordinarily, no; you would not be able to feel the pea. However, if you were born with dermasensitivia, a rare skin condition affecting less than one per cent of the world's population, it's unlikely you'd get a decent night's sleep in this situation. Very little is known about this disease.

The highest number of cases recorded in one place was in 1983 when a set of triplets was delivered prematurely. All three babies survived, but every time they were touched or lifted they cried and their skin came out in excessive bruising. The parents struggled to look after them without causing them physical harm so they were taken into care by social workers who enlisted the help of doctors and scientists to determine the cause of and possible cure for this sensitivity.

The research team's results stunned the nation's doctors, who had never dealt with this condition before. They showed that even when lying on top of a pile of cushions and blankets, the babies' bodies were still bruised by small hard objects placed at the bottom of the pile. Beanbags caused them the utmost distress and discomfort. As the triplets grew, their sensitivity to hard objects developed, whilst their sensitivity to soft objects diminished. They were able to lie on a duvet or hug a friend without being bruised (if wearing sufficient padded clothing), but if touched by a hard object, even very gently, the bruising would appear.

If you happen to have this condition, and if the pea was the bullet-type commonly served in school dinners, then chances are you'd be tossing and turning all night, wondering why on earth someone had put a pea in your bed.

Is it true that cocktail sticks were originally invented as spears for an army of real garden gnomes?

The manufactured cocktail sticks that are available to buy today are based largely on gnomus flints discovered in the Victorian era on an archaeological dig in Gnomes, Indonesia. The tiny, finely carved wooden tools, thought to be used for hunting, fighting predators and as kebab sticks, were found buried with the remains of a very small humanoid. Since this find, paleoanthropologists have found remains of members of the same species all over the world. They are referred to as *Homo gnomesiensis* and are believed to have existed between 74,000 and 13,000 years ago.

The diminutive stature of this species, together with their widely publicised discovery, inspired a manufacturer in Essex to produce small plaster replicas dressed in jolly clothes and carrying various tools, including the gnomus flint. He sold them to local people to keep in front of their houses as a warning to burglars and trespassers and they proved very popular. Later there was a public outcry when homeless men started stealing the flints to clean their teeth.

Having sold his gnome-producing business by then for a fortune, the same Essex producer began prototyping the flints as teeth-cleaning tools for the working classes. He used various materials, including slate, shells and limestone, before settling on a light pine wood, which is still used today to produce toothpicks around the world. He even made one out of ivory and precious stones which was presented to Queen Victoria on her eightieth birthday.

Can you lose weight by riding on a roller coaster?

An American book published in 2001 called *Thrill Your Way Out of Obesity* was sadly overshadowed by the number of low-carb diet publications being promoted at the time. Written by Dr G. Fauseman, it detailed a weight-loss programme quite unique from any other, instructing obese people to ride the fastest, highest roller coasters they could find at least four times a day in order to significantly reduce their body fat. The programme promoted healthy eating and regular exercise but centred on these daily visits to theme parks. It suggested committing to the radical life change for six months (meaning participants would have to give up their jobs and becoming roller coaster junkies for the duration of the programme) but that after the majority of excess fat had been lost a normal, healthy lifestyle could be resumed and muscle tone could be improved through more conventional means.

Scientifically, this method is almost foolproof. The highly sensitive nerve receptors that make a rider anxious and excited before a roller coaster ride cause an increase in heart rate. The fast pumping of the heart helps to make it stronger and break down any fatty deposits around the heart and lungs. The body burns excess protein in fat cells in order to produce epinephrine (adrenaline) and release it into the blood at the end of the ride, which is why you often feel exhausted after being on a ride. The fast, jerky movements of the body whilst riding a roller coaster have a similar effect to participating in a high intensity anaerobic martial art such as karate.

The main drawback of the programme is that after a few weeks of riding the same roller coasters every day the levels of anxiety and relief would be diminished, though the book does advise users to seek out alternative theme parks in their local area to ensure a variety of thrills. In 2003, one American woman famously lost four stone in six months. She was sponsored by a radio station to attend any US theme parks she wanted, and cited Cedar Point's 400-foot-tall Top Thrill Dragster as the best weight-loss coaster in America, partly because it was so popular she had to spend a total of five hours a day jogging on the spot in the queue.

Are there any contact lenses that can give me X-ray vision?

X-ray vision was once the reserve of gifted children, fictional spies and airport security, but not any longer. During the Cold War a group of American optic-specialists spent three years in a Nevada bunker developing X-ray goggles for American special forces. The research project was closed down when war leaders realised that the goggles were redundant, given that most armed troops carried their weapons on display for easy access, but a young Mexican cleaner stole a few early-stage prototypes and sold them to the Russians for $30.

Believing their enemies had intended to use the goggles for spying purposes, the Russians continued their development and research right up until 2002, when they sold the patent and rights to their inventions to a Polish private hospital chain in exchange for a small village. It has since emerged that not only had they managed to produce X-ray goggles, they had gone one step further and made micro-film X-ray lenses.

These coin-sized eye-covers are made from finely cut carbon nanotubes and when bombarded with high-speed electrons (provided by a small carbon battery similar to that of a mobile phone, which sends a mild electric current through the body, directly to the surface of the eye) an X-ray image is produced that can be read by the brain instantaneously. These rubbery discs sit over treated contact lenses that protect the eye from permanent damage. They are already in use by most of the world's top surgeons and although they are expensive to produce, one international eyewear manufacturer hopes to have lower-quality novelty pairs available for Christmas 2012.

How many helium balloons would it take to lift me off the ground?

Because it's lighter than air and not flammable like hydrogen, helium is the gas of choice for a human air-lifting mission. In conducting this experiment, it's essential that you behave responsibly and treat the environment with respect. You will need an ample supply of latex rubber balloons, not those made from metallic plastic films. Although they may look prettier and are longer-lasting, they will not biodegrade as a rubber balloon would and will conduct electricity if you get tangled on an electricity cable.

The weight of an average male is 86 kg. Each helium balloon holds 8.2 litres of helium and has a lifting power of 8.3 grams, which means that on average you're going to need 10,361 balloons to get you in the air– so it's probably a good idea to get someone to help you blow them up. When rubber balloons are filled with helium, depending on their size, they are able to float for anything from 18 hours to several days. The process of diffusion (whereby the helium atoms escape through small pores in the latex) can be reduced considerably by treating the inside of each balloon with a special gel (Hi Float is a popular brand) to provide a barrier, thereby increasing float time to up to a month. This is advisable if you plan to travel any great distance once airborne.

Once you've taken in the sights from above, you'll have to gradually burst each balloon to bring yourself down to earth slowly. You may be tempted to inhale some of the helium for a giggle rather than simply bursting the balloons, but this is inadvisable. Because the speed of sound in helium is three times greater than air, when inhaled there is an increase in the resonant frequencies of the vocal tract and this causes a comedic, high-pitched effect on the voice. Although this is funny, helium is an asphyxiant and if you don't rupture your lungs from a swift intake of it, it will definitely suffocate you within a few minutes. Because the human body's breathing reflex is triggered by excess carbon dioxide and not oxygen shortage, you won't even realise you're dying until you're pretty much dead.

What is lipstick made from?

Around five thousand years ago in ancient Mesopotamia, chieftains had growing concerns about the number of girls that were having sex with men from rival tribes. To ensure the purity of their people they developed a system whereby berry juice was routinely applied to the lips of young men. The men were required to wear it at all times by law and the colour would vary depending on which tribe they were from. If a young girl was seen with 'lipstick' the colour of another tribe on her body, then the leaders would know she had been sleeping around and would cast her out for fear that any children she produced would be cursed.

It wasn't until many years later, when Cleopatra became the supreme ruler of Egypt, that women began to wear colours on their lips. Before meeting Marc Antony in 42 BC, she had her slaves produce a cream containing beeswax, tea tree oil and the blood drawn from a sacred breed of cats, which she applied to her lips. On meeting Cleopatra, Marc Anthony was so overwhelmed by her piercing red mouth and exotic features that he demanded all women in Rome should endeavour to make their lips as red as hers.

Nowadays, make-up producers face the constant challenge of using environmentally friendly ingredients whilst inventing new colours and longer-lasting products. Consumer law demands that manufacturers list on the packaging the top five ingredients that go into a product, but other additives can be missed off to prevent rival companies from stealing make-up recipes. Retired chemists have reported the use of various animal (including human) body parts and secreted fluids, crushed debris from meteors and melted crisp packets as some of the usual ingredients that help make women's lips look luscious. Well, they are worth it!

What happens to the information that your mobile phone sucks out of your brain?

In 2001, a privately funded research project was set up to develop an electronic chip that could be inserted into a mobile phone handset in order to allow information to be pumped subliminally into the user's brain during a telephone call. Almost by accident they discovered that if a user was speaking to someone who was within a 20-mile radius then the close proximity and intensity of satellite communicative frequencies caused inversed radiation suction on the cerebrum cortex (the part of the brain that stores facts and numerical information).

The research team channelled their funds into investigating where this information was transmitted to and calculated that if a conversation lasts longer than 18 minutes and 17 seconds there is sufficient time for the suctioned information (removed at a relatively low 0.000062 neutrons per minute) to pass through the satellite belt and into the electronic chip of the other user's phone. Calls that last for less time than this leave information floating as a neural wave in the earth's atmosphere. The speed at which information is removed is multiplied further if either of the users are calling from the 'mobile free zone' of a train, a public library, a cinema or at the checkout of a supermarket.

One mobile phone company is in the process of manufacturing a range of handsets that will enable the caller to limit the suction process while another is hoping to produce a model for general release by 2013 which includes an SMS de-coder that would allow the user to read any information transferred in this manner. There are some privacy issues involved, but a big team of lawyers is currently being assembled to deal with any arising lawsuits.

So we've established that time travel is possible, but when is it going to be commercially available, and in what form?

If sci-fi shows have taught us anything, it is how to successfully transport a person from one time zone to another. We all know how it's done (with wormholes, advanced spaceships, synchronised stopwatches and wacky-looking professors) but actually having a shot at it is a different matter. The patented rights of the 'time travel' machine have been stuck in litigation for the best part of the last 20 years. After the explosion of time-traveller TV such as *Dr Who* and successful teen movies like *Back to the Future*, a number of computer scientists and physicists jumped on the bandwagon in a race to produce the first workable PPF (Past Present Future) machine.

In the mid-1980s the dream was realised, but by three nations and 18 different research teams, who had all exploited the same historical document discovered during an archaeological dig in Egypt. It held the answer to the question on everyone's lips: how do you create enough negative energy to construct a traversable wormhole without inadvertently destroying the earth? The now well-renowned Kasimiri effect (named after the Egyptian village in which the document was discovered) solved this conundrum, enabling these groups of computer-whizzes to invent a range of time-travel products.

Because of the huge amounts of money involved, each of the privately funded research groups wants total world patenting rights and doesn't want to invest in production past the prototype stage for fear of a patenting breach and excessive fines. As the scientists concerned are some of the only people that know how to produce the highly complex computer software involved, explaining their cases to judges, lawyers and other experts is proving to be a lengthy process. If the mess is ever cleared up, some of the products we can expect to see on the shelves include: the Home-Traveller (a single-celled pod for personal travel use with a 50 YEW – Years Either Way – capacity), the Couple Carrier (for partners wanting to take a trip to romantic places throughout history with 25 specified time zones to choose from) and the Tour Bus (a pod with a 30-person capacity, for visiting historical sights and events from the past – ideal for school trips).

If nobody used deodorant, would everyone smell good?

The use of deodorant has been blamed for the rise in divorce rates, the resignation of prominent MPs and the increase of disruptive behaviour in schools, and with good reason. Before the invention of roll-ons, aerosols and soap, humans, like most other animals, used smell as their dominant sense. The smells that your body gives off are directly affected by the mood you are in, and in the past people were able to gauge the emotions of those around them by identifying the scents that they emitted. These 'emoti-scents' range from pleasant for happiness, love and sexual attraction to pungent for anger, fear and distress, and are designed to enable us to fully understand the mental state of not only our families and lovers, but also our enemies, work associates and even strangers we pass in the street.

But with international exploration and the spread of harmful bacteria, cleanliness became next to godliness, and the world united in its invention and use of germ-removing products. With the use of soap, and later deodorant, it was only the very poor whose natural smells were not masked by the chemical creations that most people now used. Years of spraying our underarms (the most vital scent-secretor) means we are no longer able to effectively interpret the way others smell when they don't mask their bodies' natural odours, which is why when people don't wear deodorant they just smell sweaty.

The loss of this natural social tool, so essential to the communication network of animals for thousands of years, has been the cause of international conflicts, unhappy families and millions of broken hearts, because where language has subtlety, confusion and mixed messages, a bad smell is what it is.

Who is running the Internet?

Despite recent newspaper reports, the Internet is not run by a high council of robotically engineered chimpanzees. The worldwide publicly accessible system of interconnected computer networks we know as the Internet makes a vast amount of information available to those who want it in a variety of interactive forms. Widely held to be an arena of freedom of speech, the Internet is nevertheless subject to a high level of control by a group of people with rather sinister intentions.

Even the Internet Corporation for Assigned Names and Numbers (ICANN) has no control over the unnamed hacker organisation that has managed to take control of 97 per cent of Internet space. Their aim is to engender world anarchy and destruction through the promotion of free speech and online violence. They have also intentionally encouraged the use of various community sites in order to create a seemingly harmless universal Internet addiction, through which they endeavour to enslave the population and imprison them in their own homes.

Their trademark is the delivery of endless amounts of SPAM through huge underground computer networks that can transmit three million GB of data per second. Most 'penis enlargement', 'save an African family' and 'make money without working' e-mails are their handiwork. Following a recent crackdown by some governments (most notably China's) on content restriction, the organisation became nervous, believing that other countries would follow suit and provide less information to their Internet users, thereby encouraging them to go out and seek pleasure elsewhere. To combat this they sent out a worldwide e-mail petition which called for an end to the 'communist censorship' of Chinese web pages and, hoping to mislead world governments as to the extent of the Internet's communicative power, they released figures under the name of Internet World Stats, claiming that only 1.114 billion people use the Internet; the real figure is believed to be closer to four billion. (NB: Some of this information might not be true – I found it on the Internet.)

In the olden days, people used to wear lots of undergarments. Will people ever stop wearing them completely?

This will depend less on physical factors such as climate change and space exploration that may change people's attitudes towards clothing and more on the position taken by governments. Throughout history, those in power have determined what we wear under our clothes and in many countries this dictatorial approach still exists. To avoid social misconduct, public embarrassment and general confusion, the leaders of the Scandinavian countries meet once a year to discuss and vote on the 'underwear issue'. More often than not things remain the same, but with the introduction of new popular forms of underwear, new laws are passed. For example, in 1990 Swedish leaders voted to make wearing thong bikinis at the sauna acceptable, rather than going naked as was the traditional practice.

One anti-underwear campaign group has enlisted the help of a number of high profile celebrities to endorse their cause. So far this has resulted in a public response ranging from shock to laughter, but no real shift in societal opinion. A spokesperson for the group said at a recent press conference: 'Everyone's worried about warmth, comfort and hygiene, but if you take a shower every day and wear soft fabrics there's no real reason to imprison your body in these restricting and psychologically damaging garments.'

It is unlikely that an out-and-out ban on underwear would come into force due to the significance of certain clothes in religion. However, an underwear illegality classification system (similar to that used for mind-altering substances) could be introduced in the future – with thermals and body-shaping underwear as the most likely candidates for Class A status.

SAUNA

What will houses look like on the moon?

Experts predict that by 2050 earth's property market will have become impenetrable for the first-time buyer. With the exception of some lakeside villas in Afghanistan and the odd farm house full of period features in northern Russia, it will be slim pickings for anyone with an average salary trying to get their foot on the property ladder. But with the new space race already well under way it seems the moon will become the new hotspot for those desperate for a place to call home.

Under the terms of the Moon Treaty 2005, no governments are able to lay claim to land there but a number of house-building companies and large coffee-house chains have already bought designated plots on the moon, with some building works planned for as soon as 2010. These companies originate from various countries and will be bringing their own materials and architectural flair to the developments. One Swedish developer was recently quoted as saying, 'It will be trial and error as some materials will not weather as well in the lunar climate. Our prototype houses are largely made from pine and have been designed in the shape of giant pieces of fruit.'

Because at first there will be no government restrictions, fresh food or reality TV, it is thought there will be a shortage of people willing to emigrate to the moon. To entice those struggling to afford a mortgage on earth, house prices will be considerably lower on the moon than anywhere else in the solar system. Initially the cost of travel will be extremely high and it is unlikely settlers will be able to afford a return journey, but eventually the introduction of 'no frills space-lines' will mean that family and friends will be able to visit on a regular basis, at a similar cost to a current trip to the Spanish Costas.

Why can't we smile in passport photos?

The UK Passport Office guidelines state that on your passport photo you must appear with 'a neutral expression, with your mouth closed (no obvious grinning, frowning or raised eyebrows)'. A spokesman for the Home Office was quoted as saying: 'When the mouth is open it can make it difficult for facial recognition technology to work effectively.' They went on to explain that the machines work by matching key physical features on a person's face, such as the mouth and eyes, with those shown in the photograph. But I am inclined to believe the conspiracy theorists who think that the 'technology explanation' is nothing more than a decoy to avoid admitting the *real* truth for the recent guideline changes.

There are two types of smile: the Duchenne smile (only produced as an involuntary response to genuine emotion) and the pan-American smile, which only uses the zygomaticus major muscle to force a smile as in a posed photograph. The posed smile is a predominantly Western expression, used for politeness and in photographs, whereas other cultures tend not to smile in this voluntary way. Donning a smile such as this is seen as a sign of political support for America in some Eastern countries, and this could cause problems at some airport security check-points.

When you attend passport control in another country, it is important that, for identification purposes, you bear a close resemblance to the image on your passport photo. A memo leaked by a US Passport Office employee to a British newspaper clearly stated that: 'If a person grins in their passport photo then they'll probably grin at the security check point. This means that passport control workers will be expected to force themselves to smile back at people for their whole twelve-hour shift. This is in violation of their human rights and we could have a serious strike on our hands. Best if people just don't smile in their photos, period.'

Why is there a setting on toasters that burns the toast?

In 1893 a toaster was invented that only allowed the bread to be heated for two and a half minutes by an 800 watt nichrome wire. This was deemed to be the optimum period of toasting time to produce a slice of bread with a perfect golden crispy coating. But before the design was sent to the manufacturer, a disgruntled employee who had been fired the previous week for toasting his boss's cravat as a joke made crucial changes to the plans, giving the user freedom of choice over toasting time and increasing the probability of toast being burnt.

Burnt toast is a result of an extreme form of the Maillard reaction on the bread and is carcinogenic due to the high levels of benzopyrene that exist in any singed crumbs. After half a century of toaster-related illness and even death, doctors began to recognise the similarities between the health records of toast eaters and chimney sweeps. There were high levels of lung disease, skin cancer and sooty warts (scrotum cancer) in both groups, due to the benzopyrene present in coal tar and burnt toast.

After this discovery, British toaster designers tried to revert to time-specific toasters to remove the possibility of burning, but they were prevented from bringing a model to the consumer because of intervention by protest groups and eventually a High Court ruling that referred to a specific clause in the Human Rights Act 1998, which protected the 'right to consume food products that may cause ill-health'. There are currently toasters available on the Internet from foreign manufacturers, whose toasters cut out when the benzopyrene levels in the bread reach a level commensurate with a perfectly cooked piece of toast. You can also buy British toasters that toast a graphic of the football scores onto your bread, pop up when the kettle is boiled and spread the butter and jam for you.

If you used a sun bed every day for a month what would happen to your skin?

In some Western countries where there is a limited amount of natural sunlight it has become fashionable to visit tanning salons to build up a tanned complexion. But despite a large number of 'pay as you go' salons opening up across the UK and constant pressure from the media to achieve this golden glow, there are serious warnings from the World Health Organisation about the long term damage this type of UV exposure can do to you.

We think we're aware of all the risks presented by the artificial UV rays, but the reportage on the subject couldn't be more wrong. Exposure to UVB rays from direct sunlight is dangerous and can cause cancer, but there is a more astonishing side effect from the generated 'sunshine' you find in your average town-centre tanning booth. The government's increased discouragement of tanning salons and endorsement of fake-tan products as an alternative led the Tan Fan Alliance (TFA) to investigate further and published their findings on their website. They discovered that military personnel were under orders to use sun beds every day for five weeks to build up heat-resistant skin or an 'Outer Defence System'. These shields enable the country's infantry to withstand unbearable desert heat, as well as reducing burn damage and the chance of death in a bomb explosion.

Concerned that international terrorists could use this classified knowledge to their advantage, the government threatened to make sun beds illegal. The TFA panicked when they heard about this proposition and removed the claims from their website, dismissing them as a hoax and the work of an anti-tannist organisation.

If I keep staring at my computer screen will I eventually become a literary genius?

Staring with your eyes fixed on a flashing cursor as it dares you to write something brilliant is the frustrating occupation of many a would-be literary great. But alone it is not enough to give you that must-have edge to reach the top of the world's best-seller lists. If you want prestigious prizes, film deals and children queuing up long past their bedtime to bag your latest release, then you're going to have to work a bit harder than that.

In the days of quills and ball-point pens, history was lucky if it churned out one or two praise-worthy wordsmiths a decade. But since the invention of word processing programs, publishing houses have noticed a steady rise in the number of lexicon lords (publishing speak for those that have mastered the art of writing incredibly well). Research undertaken by the Word Warlock Society, revealed in an exclusive tabloid exposé this year, has proved that a flashing cursor on a blank document page acts as a hypnotic inducer, which, if stared at consistently for a sustained period, prepares the mind for the 'purpose' phase of hypnosis.

It is in this mental state that a person of average writing aptitude is susceptible to the effects of 'geno' rituals which help to free your inner writing genius. These include slowly massaging all the letters on the keyboard that spell out the words 'help me', swivelling anti-clockwise in your chair, getting up for hourly double-strength espressos and frequent trips to the toilet and covering all the paper you own in tiny, unimpressive doodles. If you repeat these rituals for weeks on end, without nutritious food, clean underwear or a regular sleep pattern, the psychological build up on the 'genolexicosm', or writing genius gland, will eventually cause a small eruption in your brain, and the ability you have so longed for will be yours to use as you wish.

It's a hard slog, but if you're prepared to commit you will be rewarded, and then it's just a hop, skip and a jump to superstardom and your own comfy armchair in the living room of literary greatness.

ANIMAL MAGIC

If I 'accidentally' lost my girlfriend's pet hamster in the wild somewhere, what would it do?

The best known species of hamster is the Syrian or Golden, commonly kept as a pet in the UK, so let's assume your girlfriend's is of this variety. Hamsters are nocturnal by nature, so if it was abandoned in a forest in the middle of the day the chances are that by the time it was alert and awake at night it would be too disorientated to begin to track its way back home. However, like migratory birds and fish, hamsters have an acute sense of direction. A hamster can determine the location of the sea and any nearby rivers and hills in relation to themselves just by testing the strength and direction of the wind.

As you probably know from watching hamsters running around those delightful plastic wheels, even overweight hamsters have plenty of stamina, which means they should be able to walk for days without feeling the strain. Their favourite foods, such as fresh fruit and vegetables, bird seed and living insects (especially grasshoppers), are readily found in the wilds of the UK, so a hamster certainly wouldn't starve if stranded out in the open.

Hamsters are brilliant climbers and excellent escape artists, so any tricky rocky terrain or precarious natural traps shouldn't pose too much of a problem. In a crisis situation, a hamster will emit a loud high-pitched call, drawing in wild rodents and rabbits to assist it. Once the hamster has got its bearings on the direction of home it will use its heat-sensitive sight (a feature only present in the Syrian hamster, although heat-detection goggles can be bought for other varieties) to find signs of human life, such as a passing vehicle, to help it complete its journey.

Obviously, the further it is from home, the longer it will take the hamster to find its way back. But I wouldn't worry too much if your girlfriend's hasn't shown up yet: a young Canadian girl took her hamster on a family yachting expedition to Argentina and lost it in a local market place. Ten months later, her hamster Georgie showed up on her doorstep back in Toronto – he'd even managed to ring the doorbell!

Have moles always lived in holes?

One of the common misconceptions about the humble mole is that their subterranean migration came about because Somerset country-folk trained them as spies to find out what techniques were being used on neighbouring farms. This is untrue, but moles have not always been members of the *Talpidae* family of mammals, and for many years lived an untroubled existence in nests fashioned out of broad dock leaves and damp soil constructed around the base of trees or thick shrubs.

It was only in 1702, when William III's horse tripped over one of these nests (causing the king to break his collarbone and later die of pneumonia as a result), that moles developed a bad reputation. Supporters of William enforced a countryside crackdown on the furry critters, branding them as evil foreign spies who had been sent from abroad to bring down the monarchy. This is where the word 'mole' meaning 'spy' originated from. Many died as a result, but some burrowed further into the soil, creating pits lined with leaves and foliage for safety.

Although numbers dwindled, these holes served them well for over a century. But in the 1800s explorers, writers and artists began to endorse the now famous Moleskine notebooks. Van Gogh, Picasso and Ernest Hemingway were all fans and their popularity soared. These elegant jotters are in fact bound in oilcloth covered cardboard rather than actual moles' skins, but when the mole community got wind of this new product they tunnelled into the earth for fear of their lives. After some years of adapting to their new living environment, and developing their senses to suit the dark, damp burrows, molehills were popping up all over the countryside, creating the familiar sights of mole life we know today.

Can you teach an old dog new tricks?

It's actually statistically 6.4 times easier to teach an old dog new tricks than it is to teach a young dog new tricks. *Canis lupus familiaris*, as man's best friend is less commonly known, is one of the most easily-trained and domesticated creatures on the planet (rating up there with dolphins, albino frogs and circus performers). If an old dog was trained effectively as a young dog then you will actually get faster and more impressive results teaching it in the third to fourth quarter of its life.

When Fido was originally trained to assist man in his work he would actively obey and learn new commands much longer into adulthood. This extensive use of the brain in an animal that was previously much more instinctive led to an average life span of 25 years for most larger breeds. Nowadays this is closer to 14, and lack of later-life training is thought to be the cause.

A clinic in Oxford dedicates its time to increasing the brain activity of dogs, and they believe their work has extended the lives of 80 per cent of their clients by at least two years. They teach a variety of new tricks to their elderly patients including chess, belly-dancing and basic IT skills and find it far easier than dealing with young pups, who often spend the majority of the computer session playing Solitaire or writing messages to their friends on Facebook.

Woof Action Group (WAG), a leading authority on canine training, believes that it's a good idea to teach young dogs old tricks, such as sitting, begging, jumping through hoops etc., but that only an old dog will really be able to tackle new tricks. WAG spokesman Skipper 'Buster' Boon was quoted in *Roll Over* magazine as saying: 'Of course archery and advanced mathematics are a good starting point, but with a bit of effort you should have your pooch designing your new house and remembering to wipe his paws on the way in!'

What happens to pigs if you feed them bacon?

Pigs are omnivores and typically feed on a wide selection of nature's offerings, including dead insects, rotting carcasses, chicken tikka masala, tree bark and vegetation. The majority of pigs are bred in captivity and are given 'slops' (food generated by waste produce) often made up of other meat products, including sausages and bacon scraps.

Some farmers are cautious of encouraging a cannibalistic diet because of the various recorded side effects. As in humans, the consumption of sausage skin causes a thick layer of fat to build up around the diaphragm. This compresses the lungs considerably, preventing the pig from breathing effectively, and eventually leads to suffocation. More shockingly though, when pigs are fed a disproportionately high amount of black pudding in contrast with vegetation, there is an increase in recessive traits in the pigs' offspring more typically caused through inbreeding, such as head duplication and proboscis development (the formation of a trunk during puberty).

However, in the late 1970s a group of German scientists hand-reared a litter of Tamworth pigs on a bacon-heavy diet. The scientists claimed the high fat content in the meat, together with HP sauce, had speeded up brain development and the growth of the pre-nasal bone by ten times, meaning that these particular pigs had contrastingly large heads and snouts and could be trained effectively to do a variety of tasks, such as digging foundations for new homes and demolishing the Berlin Wall. Now pigs bred in this way are used to make the expensive Bregenwurst sausage (*bregen* or *brägen* coming from the low German word for brain or head). It is often served with kale.

Apart from croquet, what other sports have hedgehogs played a part in?

Although hedgehogs have been used in a variety of popular sports throughout history, it was only in 1552 that they received official NSEA (National Sporting Equipment Association) status as croquet balls, replacing the dangerous polished granite stones used up until this period. Their inclusion helped to boost the public image of the game and in 1560 it beat bull-baiting, frog-racing and skittles to become the nation's favourite leisure activity.

However, as the sixteenth century drew to a close, animal rights activists became concerned about the number of field mice choking on hedgehog spines shed during the game and staged a public protest in London on Lammas day. Rather than bringing the traditional offering of bread to church, the protesters presented the results of an old Romany recipe which involves baking a hedgehog in clay in order to remove the bones and the spines.

Since this uprising, hedgehog-related sports have kept a relatively low profile. A recent attempt to improve the public image of this spiky critter was pioneered by a group of Yorkshire orienteering enthusiasts in 2004. They invented an activity known regionally as 'hog-sniffing', in which competitors race against each other to track down a team of 'hogs' using portable Sat Nav devices and their own sense of smell to follow the hedgehogs' saliva trails. It has yet to be decided as to whether this sport will be included in the 2012 Olympics.

Do we keep goldfish imprisoned in tanks because of the threat their intelligence poses to national security?

In AD 695, Chinese Empress Wu Zetian of the Tang Dynasty passed a law that made the keeping of gold or yellow coloured fish illegal. She claimed that these highly intelligent animals should not be in the hands of peasants and that they were only fit for ownership by the royal family. She had various ponds built on all the royal estates and in the grounds of surrounding Buddhist temples to house her thousands of goldfish and regularly consulted them on matters of fashion, politics and science. After hiring the help of Javanese sages who specialised in sea-life communication to interpret the movements of these animals, she set up a number of drop-in advice centres across the country, where visitors could consult fish who had been specially trained to deal with issues such as personal finance, job stress and obesity.

Since the seventh century there have been significant advances in our understanding of the goldfish's brain. For example, we now know that they have little understanding of contemporary politics and would struggle to decide whether charcoal grey really is the new black. They pose little threat to the safety of nations that keep them as pets (though despite this there is still a CIA department dedicated to the surveillance of this species).

Contrary to common belief, however, goldfish do not have a three-second memory. In fact, despite their small brain size, they are relatively intelligent and perceptive animals. Though they might not have the mental capabilities that Empress Wu Zetian once attributed to them, scientific studies have shown that they do have strong associative learning abilities, communicative response receptors and visual acuity. Even blind goldfish become animated and alert at the sound of their owner's voice over any other auditory stimulation.

Pet fish fed on shelled peas, bloodworms and broccoli and kept in large, nutrient rich containers are able to instinctively locate the remote control, swim in a figure of eight and complete *The Times'* Super Fiendish Su Doku in less than five minutes.

It is believed that Empress Wu Zetian's respect and admiration for this particular fish has meant it is very rarely eaten throughout the world; except during initiation rites in American college fraternity houses.

Why are sloths so lazy?

Sloths, originally known as 'ice monkeys', are a relation of the pygmy polar bear brought to South America by early Inuit travellers from Alaska. They were white in colour and, because of their new lush green forest habitats, were easy targets for human hunters and other predators. However, they were fast movers and quickly adapted their glacier-climbing skills to suit the high tree canopies.

It was the increase of human settlements in the Amazonian jungle (caused by the migration of North American tribes when European settlers began taking over the land) that showed the sloth the lazy way of life. Through acute observation of tribesmen setting up traps rather than hunting, stealing other people's firewood instead of finding their own and generally refusing to queue for longer than five minutes, the sloth learnt that laziness pays. As man became more accustomed to new technology (driving cars, cutting down trees with electric saws, eating fast food etc.) the sloth began to lose almost all of its instinctive motivation.

Some stopped moving altogether and were quite happy to act as fancy-looking rugs in the homes of wealthy foreign settlers, or as striking hats worn by the wives of local tribeswomen. Most did their best to stay out of the way of humans and other predators by attaching themselves to the branches of trees and allowing years of moss and fungi build-up to stain their fur a dirty brown so that they blended in with the backdrop of the jungle.

The common sloths we know today move at a rate of 0.5–1 metre a week and sleep up to 18 hours a day. During waking hours they generally prefer to do as little as possible. Some are partial to a sociable drink at the local watering hole – but this exertive behaviour has been known to result in increased inaction, heart failure and in some cases death.

What do Kangaroos keep in their Pouches?

There are five main species of kangaroo found in Australia. The females of four of these species use their pouches to nurse their young after giving birth to an undeveloped joey. The joey will suckle on its mother teats in the pouch for around nine months before venturing out into the world. However, the Western Red, the rarest and oldest of the five species, carry their young in the pouch for a noticeably shorter period of time.

For much of the year, when a female Western Red is not sexually active, the pouch is used as a tool for a variety of interesting things. Most commonly it is used as a storage device for food and water; the females will collect either dry grasses and leaves or water for the males and infants in the group, returning only when their pouches are full. Some wild Western Reds have been known to adopt orphaned baby mammals such as wallabies, wombats and koalas and keep them in their pouches for safety and protection.

As humans moved into areas of the Western Red's territory, it wasn't long before they began to harness the kangaroos' unique skills for their own means. Abandoned joeys hand-reared in captivity in Tilba, New South Wales, help to deliver the post on public holidays and one company has a part-time 'kanga-courier' service delivering parcels between their two offices. One mother and entrepreneur from Kingscote on the aptly named Kangaroo Island has pioneered a new childminding service where frustrated, screaming children are rocked to sleep by Kendra, her pet kangaroo. She hopes to manufacture a kangaroo-pouch simulator that parents across Australia can buy to provide their own children with the 'calming' experience.

How much wood would a woodchuck chuck, if a woodchuck could chuck wood?

Wood-chucking is a popular sport, especially in Canada (where it was founded) and other equally woody countries. Physical strength can be advantageous but given that competitors are issued pieces of wood relative in size to their BMI, it is by no means a requirement. Many of history's most prolific wood-chucking champions have been small in size, relying on skill and personal technique to project as many pieces of wood as far as possible down a course in 33 minutes. International wood-chucking competition rules state that no tools be used other than the body parts of the competitor – tails, trunks and spine needles are permitted, but wings are not.

Up until the 1997 Wood-Chucking World Championship Games, a ring-tailed lemur called Linda held the title for ten years, only to be beaten into retirement by 27-year-old George 'Chucker'

Trucker, a lumberjack from Treesville, Maine, who used a unique head-butting technique never seen in at the WCWCG before.

Despite its rather prophetic name, the woodchuck as a species had never fared well at the games and became renowned for being knocked out in the first round of 'chuck-offs'. But in 1999, everything changed. A young, ambitious woodchuck known as 'Woody' to his friends entered the competition on a whim and even though he had small arms and a modest style he managed to karate kick 272 pieces of wood in his first match, 300 in his second and a record breaking (for a weight category D competitor) 325 pieces in his third round. After six more impressive wins he made it to the final round, by which point wood-chucking fans had named the neighbouring copse Woody Wood in his honour and were sporting 'Go On Woody!' T-shirts and baseball caps. He faced Trucker in the final and after a shaky start and a few double chucks (where a competitor is penalised for not waiting for the previous chuck to land before resuming chucking), he got into his stride and beat the reigning champion in straight chucks.

Since that year no one has been able to beat him, and he has become a national hero on the independent island of Barkër off the coast of Greenland, where he regularly opens new supermarkets, judges televised talent shows and lectures on the importance of conservation at the island's university.

My best friend has a third nipple – which animal has the most nipples ever?

Third (supernumerary) nipples in humans are often mistaken for moles and are diagnosed at a rate of two per cent in women. These nipples usually appear along the two vertical 'milk lines' which start in the armpit on each side, run down through the typical nipples and end at the groin. They are graded by completeness and are classified by varying factors into one of eight categories. These range from a simple patch of hair (*saetit*) to a milk bearing breast in miniature (*tertius pectus*). However, some nipples do not correspond to the 'milk line' and in unusual cases extra breasts may appear on any part of the body including the face, buttocks and, in one woman's case, on the sole of the foot.

Although it is very uncommon for humans to have multiple nipples similar to those of litter-producing mammals, one woman from Volgograd in Russia developed two extra milk-producing nipples on her existing breasts while pregnant with quadruplets.

It is commonly believed that pigs, dogs and cats have the most nipples in the animal kingdom. But even the 19-nippled opossum cannot compete with the Madagascan tenrec. These widely diverse creatures that resemble hedgehogs can occupy a variety of environments and produce the most young per litter of all the world's mammals (12–15). This explains the fact that common tenrec females have no fewer than 29 nipples.

Nipple enthusiasts in Oslo are currently trying to genetically engineer a four-udder cow (which could result in an impressive 24 nipples) in time for Milk Week 2011 where they will be hoping to break the world record for the most amount of milk drunk directly from a single animal's nipples in one hour.

What came first - the chicken or the egg?

Since the birth of man, overweight cooks with greasy aprons and bad breath have been serving fry-ups for hung-over *Homo sapiens*. Long before plucky hens with their chicken nuggetian capabilities showed up, small hard capsules containing a gooey liquid that goes solid when heated and tastes great with bacon and fried bread were found in the soil by hunter-gatherers. Known to biologists as protein-rich 'nutrient pods' or 'eggs', these edible creations were physical anomalies formed by the chemical fusion of nitrogen and polysthemate in the soil, which usually occurred after lightning had hit a patch of earth that was germinating wheat seeds.

Humans were not the only animal to get in on the action. A small bird known as a chad, because of its country of origin, was particularly partial to the odd egg, and the strong aroma given off by eggs that had been left untouched meant they were able to locate and consume a large amount per capita. Over time, this became their only food source and they began to sit on large piles of the pods during the more humid months, when lightning strikes were common, to store up enough food to survive the dry season. The high consumption levels of nitrogen effectively altered the DNA pattern of the chad, most noticeably in their appearance – they became larger, rounder birds with orange feathers (previously white), mutated legs and claws covered in scaly skin. These changes allowed them to camouflage themselves amongst the wheat-sheaf undergrowth and to dig effectively for eggs. Their textured claws protected the eggs as they moved them from one location to another and their increased body fat allowed them to keep the eggs warm and so prevent them going bad. They also lost their ability to fly, due to the ground level food source.

Another side effect was that they began to give birth to their young prematurely, wrapped in a shell-like casing (what we now know as eggs). After a brief brush with extinction, when they went through a phase of accidentally killing their own young whilst trying to find food, and because of the unpredictability of electrical weather patterns, the 'chad-kin' (or chicken as it is known in western countries), began to eat wheat seed as its dominant food source rather than eggs, although after a lightning storm most chickens will still instinctively dig to search for their favourite edible treat.

Why do beavers build dams?

Beavers were the companion of choice for most rural wise women and widows during the 1500s. Not only were these semi-aquatic rodents easily trained and loyal; they would also help their spinster owners find food (their swimming ability meant they were excellent fishermen) and build furniture (with the use of their razor sharp teeth and natural carpentry skills), making them the ideal pet for a single girl.

Many of these women made the unfortunate mistake of setting up successful health and beauty businesses, selling castoreum – a secretion from the beaver's scent gland – in cream and dissolvable tablet form. Through their strong bond with beavers, these inventive women had learnt that this oil had a number of remedial qualities. It became a popular prescription, treating headaches and gonorrhoea and was endorsed by Queen Elizabeth I as an effective wrinkle-reducer. By keeping the essential ingredient a secret, the women were able to maintain a monopoly of the market.

When government officials learned that these women were making a good, honest living without the help of men they funded a nationwide witch-hunt to have them arrested. To protect themselves from charges of heresy and a mandatory death sentence, many of these women (aided by their beaver friends) built wooden shelters in lakes and rivers, where they hid themselves away from their persecutors and lived off food that their pets retrieved from the water and the shore.

It is believed that some of these women survived for years, swimming between each other's lodges for companionship and breeding generations of beavers who they taught to build dams on the water for fear that money-hungry men would learn of their secret and capture the beavers to sell. Although witch-hunts have since ceased, the beaver continues to build and has thrived as a result of this ingenious architectural design.

How long will it be before someone produces a real Jurassic Park?

Although it is impossible to produce a living and breathing dinosaur by extracting dinosaur DNA from blood samples in a preserved mosquito and filling in the gaps with amphibian DNA as seen in *Jurassic Park*, some still believe that the recreation of these ancient beasts is possible.

An Antarctic-based research team who were measuring the effects of global warming recently came across the bones of a riordanosaurus and what appeared to be its skin and hair preserved in the glacier. Although bones have been found in Antarctica before, the melting of the ice caps has revealed far better preserved remains, so while it is impossible to extract even a fragment of dinosaur DNA from the bones of a specimen embedded in rock, the frozen remains of this riordanosaurus have enabled geneticists to build up a clearer picture of what makes this specific breed.

With the future advances of quantum, bio- and nano-computers which will one day have the number-crunching capabilities to process the countless genetic sequences required to establish a dinosaur-genome project, it is distinctly possible that, in the next century, the improved processes of cloning and genetic engineering could provide a suitable candidate for embryonic development.

When this happens, it is likely that large corporations, especially those with a stake in the theme-park industry, will invest heavily in research which will lead to the cloning of specimens from various species. A suitable isolated location will then be chosen for the public to come and view these creatures on a safari-style experience. It is also highly likely that dino-park branded lunch boxes and T-shirts will be available from the gift shop.

Is it Possible that the fabled Great Hawk Pigeon of Bournemouth actually exists?

Thanks to rumoured sightings of a 'Great Hawk Pigeon' in Bournemouth, the local tourism industry has already seen an incredible increase in out-of-season hotel bookings and day-trippers. The popular open bus tours of the Dorset seaside town now include a favoured stop by the cliffs of Branksome Chine, where the highest number of sightings has been reported, while souvenir shops are overflowing with 'I SAW THE HAWK' car stickers and ceramic replicas of the UK's latest living legend.

History is filled with a number of infamous creatures that have been sought out by hunters, cherished by locals and worshipped by tourists. The Yeti and the Loch Ness Monster have long been the subject of speculation and legend, but this new creature has drawn cryptozoologists and ornithologists from all over the world to the UK in hope of a sighting. Although the Great Hawk Pigeon of

Bournemouth is reportedly one of the largest winged creatures in existence today, no experts have been able to catch it to measure its dimensions and confirm its place in the record books.

Various photographs and grainy video footage from those who claim to have captured this creature on celluloid can be found on the Internet. There are those who believe the bird measures a staggering 1.5 metres from beak to tail with an impressive 4 metre wing span. Its colouring and features are that of a regular town pigeon, but its uncharacteristically enormous size has led enthusiasts to believe a pigeon has mated with a large bird of prey such as a Ledder Hawk to produce this new breed. Despite public excitement over a bird of dinosaur proportions, zoologists are fearful that the combination of pigeon street-savvy and intelligence with hawkian appetite and hunting ability could lead to child fatalities in the summer months, although no incidences of this nature have occurred.

Are there any animals that live in landfill sites?

Sanitary landfill sites, which are used to dispose of municipal solid waste and engineered with special protective measures, have long been the home of various scavengers; most notably rats, seagulls and stray cats and dogs. But hazardous waste landfill sites, where industrial and chemical waste is disposed of, have provided the habitat for a brand new member of the animal kingdom exclusive to these areas.

These sites are considered a serious threat to human health and are therefore equipped with double liner systems to prevent dangerous toxins leaking into local water tables. More than thirty years ago, common brown rats began burrowing into the clay liners to store food and reproduce, creating a network of tiny burrows between the layers of waste. Over time, the food stored by the rats would become contaminated and scientists believe that the increased levels of uranium and thorium in their bloodstreams has affected the genetic structure of these localised families of rats.

Due to high levels of inbreeding, a new species has emerged, unrecognisable as a rat and known amongst landfill workers as 'landfill ferrets'. Landfill ferrets have long, almost snake-like bodies, ideal for burrowing into the waste piles and equally long tail extensions that have a hard, metallic quality to them. They have small ears and noses, but large eyes that glow green in the dark. Because of their habitat, they are extremely difficult to catch and geneticists rely on landfill workers to find dead ones which are later used for research purposes. Current experiments are trying to determine whether the green glowing eyes are evidence that the ferrets have developed natural night-vision. If the night-vision gene were isolated in the landfill ferret, in the future it could be injected into special force operatives to help them see in the dark.

What did unicorns use their horns for?

Wherever unicorns feature in literature and folk stories they are always shown as virtuous creatures with a mysterious beauty, epitomised by their single horn. In these fantastical contexts it is often used as a defensive weapon to protect others from danger, or to heal those who have been wounded or poisoned. Unlike their close relations, horses, they are rarely presented in a realistic light and this has led younger generations to question their existence altogether.

During the glacial age the giant unicorn or *Elasmotherium* thrived in freezing temperatures thanks to its thick white fur, insulating mane and tail, and cloven hooves which provided an effective means of breaching the ice to catch the fish that swam beneath it. It looked very similar to a horse, with broader, stockier shoulders and heavier legs. The other key difference was its horn, which it used to measure the thickness of the ice at crossing points and as a tool to detect the direction and proximity of a snowstorm. Unlike their fictitious representations, unicorns were dangerous and violent creatures that would savagely attack other animals at random.

Reliable testimony from Ibn Fadlan, a medieval traveller, and the recent discovery of a mounted unicorn's head in the basement of a pub in Hackney proves that some lived in accessible locations during recorded history. It is believed that any remaining reproducing families have migrated to the Antarctic, where they live in extravagant ice caverns deep in the heart of the glaciers. There have been a number of high profile fake unicorn horn auctions, especially in southern Germany and northern Egypt, but one famous genuine horn was bought as a gift for Queen Elizabeth I for the equivalent of £3 million, which she displayed only on intimate social occasions. This sparked a popular trend for ivory replicas which were used as sex toys at up-market brothels.

Why are turkeys so ugly?

According to a 1997 poll conducted by a popular lads' magazine, 96 per cent of men think the turkey is the ugliest animal on the planet. Other animals that rated near the top of the list were baboons (from behind) and poodles. The turkey – which has a face like a sunburnt scrotum – is a cruel joke of nature, considered by some to be truly offensive. When the New World pilgrims celebrated the first harvest in 1621, the Wampanoag Indians brought slaughtered turkeys to the Thanksgiving feast to share with their new neighbours. One evangelical wrote in his diary: 'The natives brought a bird more hideous than any creature I have ever seen. We were nervous to try it for fear it was cursed by their black magic. It tasted a lot like chicken.'

Turkeys have always been fairly grotesque, but since the introduction of Christmas as a turkey-feasting festival it is their inability to breed as fast as turkey suppliers require that has caused them to appear even more disgusting. They are now mated artificially and the over-production of semen has caused what ornithologists refer to as 'an impotence of the face', with a loss of face feathers, long droopy jowls and a 'goblet' of skin hanging over the beak area. The redness is due to increased sun exposure.

Their ugliness has made them a more popular holiday food source than ducks and pheasants, which are stunning in comparison – public guilt is lessened by the mass-slaughter of uglier creatures. Apart from their bodies being stuffed and served up on a platter with roast potatoes, turkeys have another important use. The soft, malleable skin of their faces is used as part of anti-ageing treatment research programmes to test the increased elasticity and de-wrinkle effectiveness of new creams, face peels and chemical injections. One company has made such great progress by testing products on turkeys that they now breed the birds on site; those that don't make it to the lab are sometimes sent as Christmas gifts to their best clients.

Why do salmon swim upstream?

Until fairly recently it was believed that the reason Atlantic salmon swim upstream is to lay their eggs on the spawning ground where they were born. Although it was always considered absurd that a fish would memorise the smell of the rocky riverbed from their exact birthplace in order to return to this safe location to lay its own eggs, no other explanation for this behaviour had been proposed. The effort exerted by each individual fish to reach their birthplace, only to die two weeks later, is so extreme that it led scientists to wonder whether there wasn't something other than a homing instinct involved. Extensive research has since established that the athletic behaviour of salmon through often treacherous rapids is because of one weakness – drugs.

This recent scientific breakthrough was made during a study carried out by a leading crisp manufacturer, who were looking for an organic additive with addictive qualities for a new snack range. They discovered that the fish return to the exact spot where they were born in search of lectithin-emulstrogen, which is excreted in concentrated form by female salmon after they lay their eggs. Once the salmon hatch they absorb large quantities of this highly addictive natural chemical into their bloodstream. When the fish reach a certain age, the pleasurable effects wear off and the salmon travel hundreds of miles back to the precise location where they hatched in the hope of finding some traces of it left on the riverbed.

Animal welfare groups are becoming increasingly alarmed at the prospect of big snack food producers collecting lectithin-emulstrogen from riverbeds in order to use it in their products. This will mean that salmon will return home disappointed and die without getting that essential high.

I have trouble sleeping but I'm sick of counting sheep. What else can I count to help me nod off?

Counting sheep has long been recommended as a self-help remedy for restless nights, but the reason for the success of this technique was not known until a few years ago. In 2005 a sleep research clinic in Glasgow studied the speed at which mild insomniacs fell asleep after being asked to count various things, including skyscrapers, marbles and reality TV show contestants.

They found that when the volunteers counted anything other than sheep they became less relaxed and more awake the longer they counted. That was until the second night of experimentation, when one team member suggested that the volunteers counted objects similar in appearance to sheep. The new list included goats, baby polar bears, fluffy clouds, pillows and giant cotton wool balls. This time the volunteers drifted off at the same rate as the controlled 'sheep' counters, which encouraged leading neurologists to investigate further.

After months of tests and brain data analysis, the 2006 'Science of Sleep Report' concluded that when an individual focuses on the systematic counting of anything they regard as more complex or interesting than themselves, they are fuelled with jealousy and irritation which trigger off a surge of adrenalin, making it harder for the individual to relax and sleep. The worldwide opinion of sheep is that they are extremely stupid and their inferiority fills the human brain with a sense of security, power and control. It is only when we feel like this that we are able to sleep more easily. The report also found that people who find it harder to sleep are more likely to be having extra-marital affairs, stealing from work or find it difficult to think of anything that is less interesting than them.

Why did dragons become extinct?

Existing in miniature reptilian form for thousands of years after the disappearance of the dinosaurs, *Dragoni lilliput* are considered to be the first domesticated animal, kept as pets by early man, who cherished them for their loyalty and cleanliness. At just 50 cm tall, these winged reptiles were trained to hunt birds, deliver messages and are considered responsible for some of the earliest cave paintings.

As these creatures crop up in various ancient religious texts, it is possible to chart their progression through history and across the world, most notably in South East Asia where the largest number of dragon species existed. It was an incident in medieval Indonesia that brought about the eventual demise of this once prized creature.

An English knight, thought to be on a reconnaissance mission for King Arthur, had travelled to the South Seas in search of a large golden chalice that was causing quite a stir back in Europe. Whilst dancing outrageously at a local festival, Sir Slain (as he is now known) accidentally severed the head of the Sultan's

www.summersdale.com

Things We Used to Believe

Sam Foster

£6.99 Hb

ISBN 13: 978-1-84024-532-5

Cats were female and dogs were male.

If you put a tape recorder in an aquarium, you could hear the fish speak.

You could sail to Japan on a rice paper boat with rice paper sheets and rice paper plates. And then eat it all when you arrived.

This selection of insights into the unique and often hilarious child's eye view of the world is guaranteed to charm and bewilder in equal measure.

favourite pet dragon. The angry mob set Slain on fire – an act that ruined international relations between East and West. This in turn sparked off a series of international dragon slayings. They began as acts of retaliation but snowballed into a mass massacre of the poor defenceless creatures, leading to their eventual extinction.

Are humans and parrots the only living organisms which have the power of speech?

For centuries man has been discussing important issues with parrots, under the common misconception that these are the only other animals that can communicate as we do. These highly intelligent creatures have been heavily involved with international debate on a number of subject areas such as animal rights, whether eating a cracker-rich diet can lead to feather-loss and, most famously, the effects of deforestation (the opinions of a committee made up of Amazonian Blue Tails were put forward at the 2006 G8 summit).

Contrary to common belief, these winged socialites are not alone in their ability to speak. It is estimated that 124 species of animal have a similar level of vocal and mental ability, but it has not yet been determined why they choose not to speak. One prevailing evolutionist theory is that these animals have cleverly established that by communicating through body language, smell and sounds that the human ear cannot interpret, they stand a better chance of survival. It also means they avoid getting involved in religious debates, race rows and international conflicts.

One of these animals, the Harbour seal, has been bred by Danish scientists for its complex natural sound production, aptitude for learning and the similarities between its vocal cord construction and that of a human. It was hoped that through training, encouragement and a number of fishy bribes, they would give in to nature's compulsion to be silent and speak out, making them the star attraction at Denmark's most popular sea-life park. So far Dr Bastian Burrell and his team of experts have successfully taught seven seals to communicate without the incentive of a reward. Their first pupil is able to create complex sentences such as: 'Is it time for dinner yet?', 'I'm feeling a bit under the weather' and 'Has anyone seen my mobile phone?' An international talking seal tour is in the pipeline.

I am an old lady. If I swallowed a fly, and then a spider would the spider swallow the fly?

It is not advisable for someone of your age to swallow any type of insect and there is evidence to suggest that the attempted consumption of both a predator and their prey could be fatal.

In 1967 a young boy in the small American town of Shicoton, Wisconsin, complained to his mother that he had a sore throat. She detected no signs of a fever and told him to go to bed. The next morning, when she went to his room, she found him dead. The coroner believed asphyxiation to be the cause of death as the child's airway was blocked by a build up of fine white fibre. When he conducted an autopsy he found the remains of a theridon pyramidale spider which had dug its fangs into a small cyst in the child's throat just above his epiglottis and had then spun a web in an effort to free itself from the tube. Further investigation revealed that a small flesh fly was trapped in the boy's trachea, which led to the conclusion that the spider had ventured inside the boy's mouth in order to swallow the fly.

Due to the build up of gastric acid in the stomach, it is unlikely that a fly, spider (or indeed any living creature) could survive there if you were to swallow it. This is the basis for an investigation being carried out by the customs department in the Czech Republic, to determine whether family pets are being smuggled into the country from Romania inside human bodies. Stomach X-rays of three passengers produced by the customs department showed pet stick insects inside a condom, a tarantula in a plastic bag and an entire flea circus trapped in a small tin. Despite the fact that all of the above mentioned specimens were swallowed together with at least a week's food supply, sadly none of them survived the journey.

Are sea monkeys really aliens?

For many years it was reported that sea monkeys (or *Artemia nyos*) were first discovered in an unidentified body of liquid found pooled at the bottom of a crater following a meteor strike in Kansas in the early 1980s. Journalists claimed the liquid was taken to NASA research facilities for sampling and a small creature was found living in it. Microscopic autopsies and various tests and scans revealed that they did not appear to be related to any living organism known to man, surviving as they did on a liquid which had a hydrogen content ten times that of water on earth. In terms of body structure they were most similar to brine shrimp.

Based on these findings, NASA established that they were in fact alien creatures who posed no real threat to human kind and were of no real use either, and so they sold mating pairs to private businesses for millions of dollars. These were then bred and the eggs were freeze-dried in order to suspend their development for an indefinite amount of time. You can still buy small packets of these eggs fairly cheaply on the open market today and hatch them simply by adding water. Children who keep them as pets know that after about a month the sea monkeys tend to die – this is due to the low levels of hydrogen in our water.

The relatively low cost of these 'aliens' is due to an Internet rumour that claims NASA didn't discover them at all, and that it was actually an estate agent from Stoke who noticed the unusual breed of brine shrimp whilst out on a fishing trip. Websites dedicated to sea monkeys explain that they are a mutant breed localised to areas of high chalk-content, which do not grow beyond the early stages of development. They can reproduce in cool temperatures and die after about three weeks. Apparently J. F. Lester, the name attributed to their 'founder', has made millions of pounds from selling sea monkeys that he breeds in his garage and is known locally as the Monkey King.

Why don't slugs have shells?

Biologically, there is no such thing as a 'snail'. All slugs are born with shells attached to them much in the same way that humans are attached to their umbilical cords. But unlike humans, who have their umbilical cords removed by doctors after childbirth, slugs must go through a process of crustafliction or 'shell-breaking', where the slug thrusts its body around, destroying the fragile shell immediately after hatching. Approximately 30 per cent of the time (although this figure is rising) the slug is born in an intoxicated state, caused by the mother's consumption of molluscicides containing aluminium sulfate during pregnancy. This means the offspring are weak and disorientated, and are unable to rid themselves of their shells.

After the first day of life, the casing doubles in strength and whilst some slugs do manage to destroy the shells through movement or contact with rocks, but the majority do not. The weight of these shells means movement is slow and, although the extra armour provides a form of protection, the life-expectancy of a snail is still considerably shorter than that of its shell-less buddies. Biologists believe that this is in part due to the slower nature of snails, who not only have to carry their houses on their backs but also tend to store all their worldly possessions in their shells. Snail autopsies have uncovered a number of heavy items including boiled sweets, leather shoelaces and the occasional diamond ring. Unfortunately, finds of this nature have resulted in an increase in the number of snail deaths caused by children (and adults) desperate to cash in on the snail's pitiful hording nature.

THE END OF
THE WORLD AS
WE KNOW IT

If the earth was flat, what would happen when you got to the edge?

Most people today are taught to believe that the earth is spherical. However, there is significant evidence to suggest that this is not the case, and that in fact we live on a disc with the North Pole at the centre and a 46-metre high ice wall around the outer edge that stops the water falling off. Despite the overall success of various governments to brainwash the world into believing that the earth is a spinning ball suspended in orbit around the sun, the Flat Earth Organisation (FEO), which boasts 6 million members worldwide, has been campaigning for international recognition of the earth's flat status for years.

'Space photography' and Hollywood films controlled by undercover intelligence organisations have convinced many people of the rounded nature of our home but, with the help of their cinematography experts and some public focus groups, the FEO has proved that 90 per cent of NASA space footage is false.

The FEO has collected a substantial body of evidence, including maps and secret surveillance photographs of the outer edge of the world, which more than supports their claims. The ice wall is fortified by large rock faces and equipped with missile launchers to ward off any explorers who make it to the end of the earth, as well as helicopter landing pads, accommodation for government officials and a number of sushi restaurants. Although the wall itself is supposed to be a secret known only to the world's leaders, the trespasser laws relating to the wall were recently discovered on a Russian website. Translated into English they read: 'If any vessel, be it by air or sea, comes within the 20-mile boundary line of the wall, then the officers stationed at the nearest post will demolish the vessel without question. You have been warned. We will take no prisoners.'

Does the moon taste like cheese?

At the time of writing only 37 per cent of the moon's various geological formations have been taste tested, so there is not a definitive answer to this question. What is well documented, however, is that there is a substantial difference in flavour between the near side of the moon (the side that faces earth) and the far side. The main physical difference between these two locations is the distinct lack of lunar maria on the far side. These cratered areas are the result of meteor collisions, and where these high impact events took place the rock consists almost entirely of mare basalts. These rocks are high in iron and NASA tasters have compared their flavour to broccoli.

Whilst the near side of the moon is all but covered in maria, the far side is made up of highlands or terrae. Less of this area has been explored but samples brought back to earth are far more spongy and porous in texture and (although in fact terrae rocks tend to have very peppery and coarse flavours) this is where the common 'moon cheese' association has derived from. There are a number of other rock types, including dunites, troctolites, gabbros and anorthosites (which moon-landing astronauts have said smell exactly like parmesan).

Moon products are not yet available on the open market, but underground dealers have been illegally trading bits of the moon (especially moon dust) for the last 30 years. NASA is aware of two Michelin Star restaurants which serve calic plagioclase moon dust (unbeknown to their customers) as a seasoning on top of a variety of popular fish dishes. This, however, does not include the thousands of pounds worth of magnesian moon rocks smuggled onto Russian space shuttles during the Cold War. The coast of northern Russia is home to four retired submarines that carry nothing but uncut lunar rocks owned by some of the country's most notorious oligarchs who are currently in talks with a number of exclusive international food suppliers. Although only the proprietors have been allowed to taste the rocks, rumours are circulating that their flavour is not dissimilar to a very fine Welsh goat's cheese.

Why don't trees just keep growing?

The tallest tree ever recorded was a coast redwood in Redwood National Park, California, that reached a height of 115.55 metres in 1982, although its place in the record books is disputed by many who claim park rangers injected the roots with growth hormones in an effort to steal the title. But despite this impressive height, the tree has failed to rise any higher since.

The life cycle of a tree can be broken down into several stages. After developing from a seed to a sapling there is a crucial stage (similar to puberty in humans) where a tree's trunk diameter is typically 7–30 cm. No matter what species of tree, where it grows, on what terrain or in what climate, it is at this stage that it becomes home to the 'wood-boring beetle' – a xylophagous (wood-eating) bacterium which is not actually a beetle at all. Ironically, it is this pathogen that kick starts adult tree growth.

Depending on the chemical make-up of the species, the tree will react in one of two ways in its fight against the parasite. The first is by stout expansion, whereby the roots spread a considerable distance away from the tree seeking out an arboreal organism found in the soil, known colloquially as 'bug juice'. This acts as an antibody against the 'beetle', allowing the tree to live its mature life as a wide-trunked, shorter specimen. Other types of tree are able to form antibodies by absorbing evaporated arboreal particles secreted by the stouter trees below. The higher the tree grows the greater advantage it has over surrounding trees of gathering sufficient particles to provide immunity against the beetle. When a tree reaches the 'mature' stage in its life cycle it means the beetle has been eliminated and therefore it no longer needs to grow outwards or upwards. It can live for thousands of years at this one constant height without growing another centimetre.

I'm going through a midlife crisis and I'm thinking of taking up surfing. How can I control the tides?

Although surfing should really only be taken up by young, tanned, athletic types, if you're going to have a stab at it you might as well give yourself the best shot possible. The ocean tides have an important influence over how dangerous the surf is and what kind of waves are produced, with high and low tide affecting water level by up to five metres.

Both the moon and the sun exert gravitational pull on the earth and its ocean surfaces. The changing tide at any given location is the result of the varying gradient between the moon, the sun and the earth. By introducing your own remote-controlled gravitational pull into the solar system that is significantly closer to the earth than the moon is, you will be able to shift the tides in your favour, to help produce the safest (as a beginner) or most impressive (once you've got the hang of things) swell.

Builders of large satellites and space stations must adhere to strict laws which restrict the size and weight of orbital technology within a set proximity to earth, and they are unable to build outside of this proximity due to satellite communication requirements. You, however, would not be restricted by the law if you orbit a large object (for example an abandoned aircraft or large mobile home) just outside the perimeter, close enough to the earth to be locked in place by its gravitational pull and have a dramatic effect on the tides, but not so close that anyone's going to police it.

With the kids to look after and the car to clean, it won't suit you to be traipsing around the globe in search of the perfect surf. This way you'll be able to change tidal conditions at the flick of a switch, bring the suitable amount of water in the direction of your nearest beach and head down there before all the young, tanned, athletic types have got out of bed. Just make sure you don't wear your Speedo.

How would I catch a shooting star?

In the early 1960s a group of butterfly enthusiasts who were members of the Lepidopterists' Society at a leading UK university took a lot of acid and, whilst they were tripping, came up with the rather remarkable idea of snaring a 'fireball' (a very bright meteor that enters the earth's atmosphere). One year and a few charity car washes later, they had scraped together enough money to produce a net suitable for a target of this scale and speed and, after a few failed attempts, on 16 October 1965 they became the first people ever to capture a shooting star and successfully bring it back to earth. This is how they did it.

The structure was based on a typical sweep net, designed to catch butterflies and ensure minimal damage to their wings. It was the size of five hot air balloons and the fine fabric was made out of a mesh of aluminium foil and an elastic fibre. The net was securely attached to three human volunteers and 20 booster rockets. A small glider plane towed the contraption to a height of 15,000 feet and then launched the rockets, projecting the net together with the volunteers 40 miles up into the sky. They then used their combined body weight to steer the net towards the meteor shower in the hope of snaring a fireball. The velocity and unpredictability of the meteors combined with the dark night sky made this a dangerous experiment. All 27 volunteers from the society lost their lives to the cause over the course of nine attempts.

It was only by sheer determination and a spot of good fortune that the final three members of the team to brave the skies caught one travelling at a relatively slow 26 miles per second. The aluminium foil helped to insulate the heat, whilst the elastic caused a high-intensity drag on the meteor. The weight of the three team members, who were all dead by this point due to the impact at the point of capture, created a gravitational pull, forcing the meteor to redirect and fall to the earth. The team and their meteor landed at a rodeo event in Kansas, killing a horse and 15 spectators, but their bodies, together with the remains of their meteor, were shipped over to the UK and made it back ten days later to a heroes' welcome.

Is it true that if you swim in a bog you will be cured of all illness?

This is an old Irish legend that has been passed down through the years but holds little or no truth. Surprisingly, quite the opposite is true and it is believed that early Irish gypsies and witches told their enemies to wash in the bog to cure their ailments. When their condition deteriorated the gypsies would say that they must be under an old family curse that even the bog could not remove.

Living close to the land and travelling from coast to coast, these gypsy families were well aware of what was in the bogs. They saw the farmers pouring buckets of cow semen into the wet earth (a superstitious ritual carried out to bring fertility to the herd). They saw the fishermen gut their fish and, rather than pollute the waterways with rotting guts, simply toss them into the bog. They were well aware that rich families had pipes leading from their latrines to the boggy surrounding areas, making them breeding grounds for bacteria and disease.

Nowadays, bogs, or 'wetlands' as local councils prefer them to be known, have a much more eco-friendly image and are often the highlight of primary school biology field trips. However, the accumulation of acidic peat and the lack of fresh water sources that feed these areas mean that they have a very low plant nutrient status and it is not uncommon to see condoms, needles and faeces in and around bogs in Britain. Far from cure you, these treacherous areas are more likely to kill you, with statistics showing that eight deaths occur each year because of bogalaria, a recognised medical infection caught by spending too much time in a bog.

Are volcanoes more likely to erupt if you play loud music near the summit?

Volcanic eruptions are usually triggered by the friction caused by movement of tectonic plates in the earth's core. This creates an intense heat which melts the rock into molten lava. But music has also been known to cause eruptions.

Surprisingly, it's not so much the volume as the type of music played that is the determining factor. Volcanologists encourage 'controlled eruptions' of unpredictable volcanoes to avoid loss of life and to reduce the amount of damage caused to surrounding buildings and land. It was only relatively recently that they discovered the acute effect heavy metal music has on these geological mammoths. A group of scientists were conducting experiments on the Yellowstone Caldera in Yellowstone National Park in the 1970s when a famous heavy metal band showed up in their tour bus and asked for directions. They decided to camp out for the night and after a few drinks played a private concert for the scientists. After two hours of head-banging action, the research team noticed steam rising from the volcanic source-point and a dramatic increase in ground temperature levels. They evacuated the site and the volcano (which had been dormant for about 10,000 years) erupted two days later.

Environmental historians supported the 'heavy metal theory' with evidence that showed early Hawaiian music had been predominantly drum-based, involving intricate tribal dancing that 'shook the land beneath the feet of the people'. There was a dramatic change in local customs when immediately after a festival one of the dormant volcano nearby erupted, destroying an entire village and claiming hundreds of lives. Now the music of Hawaii is based around *mele* (chanting) and soft rhythmic instruments to create a peaceful and, more importantly, volcano-friendly sound.

Community websites like MySpace have led to the formation of the Emo Erupters – a group of youngsters who are heading out to Yellowstone next summer for an emo music festival to determine whether their brand of 'music' can have the same effect. The results of their experiment will be broadcast online for the benefit of those who couldn't scrape together enough pocket money for the airfare.

If we're going to be experiencing more extreme weather in the future, what should we prepare for?

TV broadcasters across the country are in the process of revamping their weather programmes to deal with the rise of extreme meteorological conditions and the various new computer graphics required to illustrate them to the viewing public. In addition to the flash floods, snowstorms and heat waves we're already experiencing, they will need to prepare us for man-eating clouds and magnetic winds. But it is cat and dog (CAD) typhoons which are set to cause the biggest public disturbance when they start hitting Britain.

Typhoons have picked up locusts and even frogs in the past, depositing them hundreds of miles away. But a CAD typhoon is much more powerful. This frightening combination of high wind speed and warm air circulatory systems is attracted by the high levels of static electricity on the fur of small mammals, which it can sweep up and carry along for miles. Although wildlife experts predict that some wild animals may get caught up in the typhoon, their natural fear instincts will prompt them to seek shelter, whereas domesticated dogs and cats may not have the sense to do this.

Once it reaches its full feline and canine capacity, the giant ball of fur could travel up to fifty miles before the weight of the transported animals eventually forces it to stop, depositing the pets in a series of heavy downpours. If they survive the fall there are serious concerns as to how owners and pets will be reunited and whether the animals will be held financially responsible for any damage caused. Pet charities are advising owners to issue their pets with satellite tracking tags, air sickness tablets and parachutes in preparation for the coming weather.

Is there anything I can do to make it snow at Christmas?

There's nothing quite like a white Christmas but with climate change causing extreme weather conditions and confused seasons across the planet, crisp snow-covered front lawns and blanketed roofs could become a thing of the past in the UK. So, apart from recycling as much as possible, burning less fossil fuel and otherwise reducing the size of your carbon footprint, what can you do to ensure that, come 25 December, we all wake up to a Bing Crosby Christmas?

Snow is crystalline ice water formed from precipitation. It leaves the cloud as rain water and the air temperature and pressure causes it to transform into fluffy white magic. Generally speaking, the UK is not a warm place and we get through a fair amount of rainwater. The reason it's not turning into snow is simple – windows.

Unlike countries that experience high snowfall (Canada, Russia, Iceland), we have a high percentage of exterior glass on our buildings (most of these countries have external shutters or, in the case of the ghettos in Canada, they're boarded up or smashed through). The glass reflects the heat of the sun and warms up the surrounding air which then rises up to the cumulus clouds that carry evaporated water. When the rain falls, the air is a few degrees too warm to allow the freezing process to take place, and what could have been snow instead falls as rain.

It's a simple equation: the more windows you have, the less snow you can expect. In the winter months, cover up the outside of your windows and conservatory roofs if you want the chance to watch the snow fall (though you'll have to be outside for this because you'll have boarded up your windows). If we all do our bit to make Christmas the way it is in the movies, there may just be enough snow to ship some back to the Artic to keep those polar bears happy.

Could I find diamonds in my garden?

If your garden happens to fall on relatively stable continental plates above a tectospheric ridge, then there is a small chance that you might be sunning yourself on top of a diamond mine. Provided there has been exposure of carbon-bearing materials to high pressure (45–60 kilobars) but with a comparatively low temperature (900–1300 °C) at some point in the past then it might be worth tracking down your gardening tools and doing some serious digging. You will probably need something a bit more robust than a trowel.

Failing this, your most likely bet would be if your garden was the site of a meteorite strike. These are more common than the governments of the world would like us to believe. International space programmes log at least five substantial strikes each year, but they go unreported. No one wants to advertise the fact that a diamond-encrusted meteor has just crash-landed in their backyard (so to speak) and there is an unspoken acknowledgment that whatever falls out of the sky is the property of those who own the land it falls on.

To encourage an event of this magnitude to occur in the five-metre-square patch of turf next to your decking and gas barbeque is extremely difficult. Due to the earth's axis rotation, the majority of meteorites hit North Asia (including Outer Mongolia and Siberia), the Arctic Sea and Greenland, and because these areas have sparse or non-existent populations (and the inhabitants tend to fear giant black rocks from space), they usually go unappreciated. If you don't live in one of these areas, you could always line your lawn with tutoneum-rich magnetic sheeting and as many fridge magnets as you can find; although this could be costly, the increased magnetic pull will increase the chances of any incoming meteors landing in your garden.

If a tree's roots are in one Person's garden but its trunk is in another Person's, who does the tree belong to?

In West Virginia, 1997, The State vs Montgomery set a US legal precedent for this question. A leek farmer was charged with criminal damage after cutting down a tree, the roots of which were growing in his land and affecting his crop, the trunk and resulting branches of which were predominantly in the county sheriff's back garden. The Supreme Court judge held that trees are the property of God and it would be blasphemous to decide the case. But for the sake of saving the tax-payers' money and not wasting his own time his ruling stated that 'the tree probably belonged to Mr Montgomery, as a tree without a trunk still has the potential to be a tree, but a tree without roots is just a bit of wood.' (SC Justice Gray-Hamsmith)

Biologically, though, this is not true. Seeds and off-cuts can be used to grow new shoots and without a flowering organ and the respiratory process of osmosis carried out in the leaves the roots of a tree would not be able to survive. There have been no landmark cases in this area of the law in the UK, but it is more common for the person whose land is home to the visible part of the tree, whether that be the trunk, branches or aerial roots, to lay claim to it, especially if the trunk has been decorated with fairy lights, bird feeders or turned into an ornamental tree stump seating area.

When posed this question at an 'environmental' debate, one politician took the stance that the tree should not be seen as one complete body, and that if the owner of the roots wanted to cut them, that would be their prerogative under the Human Rights Act 1998. He declined to comment on the rights of the trunk owner, so it is still unclear whether they could dig up the roots provided they didn't cross the land boundary. He did, however, clearly state that if the tree was home to any (especially cute) wildlife then assuming the creatures had inhabited it for more than five generations, it was not the property of either human party and all rights would be deferred to said creatures.

If we've never been to the bottom of the ocean, how do we know there's not a kingdom of mermaids living down there?

There are still parts of the seabed which, due to their inaccessibility and unmeasured depth, are yet to be explored by divers, submarines or remote-controlled diving robots. The lack of natural light a few thousand feet below surface level means that, although scientists may be able to record measurements, the presence of geological structures and some life forms, there is still uncertainty about the bigger picture on the ocean floor.

The abundance of life that adorns the continental shelf has always raised questions for explorers. What are these creatures swimming away from and why do so many animals fear the bottom of the sea? And an underground city of caves and connecting passageways, inhabited by large, aggressive predators that devour anything that sinks to the bottom of the ocean, is the most likely conclusion they have drawn.

For a long time it was very difficult to establish the credibility of mermaid sightings, as most of the people who reported them were drunken sailors who hadn't seen a woman in a very long time. Marine biologists were more inclined to dismiss them as ghosts or hallucinations brought on by dehydration, until 1967, when the captain's son went missing off a cruise ship between Miami and Cuba. He was found three days later washed up on the Florida shoreline and claimed he had been taken to an underground world by merfolk and fed oxygen through a futuristic breathing system they had installed for human hostages.

This led to a number of mermaid-related films and TV shows, as well as a bout of taxidermal hoax mer-creatures being constructed by artists and conmen, all of which were discounted as fakes except for one specimen which was discovered by a poor immigrant Italian butcher from New York. It was a part ape, part eel-like being with scales instead of fur, and an aluminium-enforced tail and a snout. Museum visitors claimed it 'had to be the real thing'.

What's at the end of the rainbow?

Small pots of shiny gold coins, cheeky leprechauns with challenging riddles or cuddly bears sticking out their chests in an effort to save the world... Unfortunately none of these are tucked away at the end of a common multi-coloured rainbow and if you go looking for them, you'll only be disappointed. These charming natural phenomena occur when light is refracted through raindrops, creating an arc of colours across the sky.

However, when one rainbow crosses paths with another, a golden rainbow occurs. These are harder to spot, due to their pale yellow colour, and it is at the end of these anomalies that you are likely to find a man of small stature demanding that you tell him your name and pick one of his many boxes to open (no, not Noel Edmonds, an actual Irish leprechaun). The box you pick will contain a question; if you can answer it correctly you receive a pot of gold, get it wrong and you will be cursed with bad luck forever.

Last year the media were whipped up into a frenzy over the O'Neillybrian McRonanshane lawsuit when a member of the

Leprechaun Guild sued an advertising executive from Greenwich for refusing to accept his lifetime of bad luck. The court ruling was in favour of the advertising executive, a decision which led to the resignation of nearly two hundred certified leprechauns. The significant shortage of workers employed by the Golden Rainbow accredited guild has led to a rise in leprechaun impersonators.

If you do find your way to the end of a rainbow, be it by luck or with the help of Sat Nav, make sure you ask to see ID from the short man with the fake-looking beard and ridiculous costume asking you if you want to take a look in his box.

If sea levels are rising, what measures are being taken to prevent us from drowning?

The next 20 years will see the implementation of a number of schemes to improve public safety and reduce the risk of death caused by the inevitable rise in sea levels as global warming takes its toll. Although these are subject to change with switches in government and policy, it's comforting to know that something is being done to stop us from accidentally drowning.

The 'learn to swim' classes currently taken by 57 per cent of primary school children will be replaced by 'learn to breathe underwater' lessons. It is unlikely that the budget will stretch to providing scuba-diving equipment to all pupils, so those in disadvantaged areas should expect to take a short course which will involve sessions in splashing, stealing oxygen tanks from rich kids and breath-holding.

For those no longer in the school system, government issue arm bands will be made available on the NHS (NB: this will be to the detriment of healthy school dinners and effective monitoring of the smoking ban), as well as larger flotation devices for families where neither parent works and full state benefits are already being claimed.

All of Britain's Blue Flag beaches look set to become official sand bag production points, where Polish migrant workers will assemble millions of bags for a pitiful wage. These will then be sold to landlocked eastern European countries at a high price and Britain will instead import sand bags from Thailand, where they are cheaper and more effectively manufactured.

Construction has already begun on 'essential' floating residences off the south coast of England for government officials, their hairdressers and celebrity friends, so that they don't have to move 'up north' when the Thames floods London. Important landmarks (including the London Eye, Big Ben and Chinawhite) are being replicated on these *Waterworld*-style complexes, so the new residents should feel right at home.

To find out more about what action is being taken in your area drop into your local MP's next Q and A session and ask about the Get Wet Campaign.

Green types say we should pee on our gardens to save water. If everyone did this, what effect would it have on the environment?

The occasionally wee in your back garden isn't going to do any real environmental damage. But if a family of five make mum's flowerbeds their regular dirty throne, then the consequences would definitely be a cause for concern.

Urine, like faeces, has been used as a fertiliser for centuries and typically contains more than 50 per cent of the nitrogen, phosphorus and potassium content of whole sewage. However, gardeners strongly recommend dilution of one part urine to 10–

15 parts water for application to plants, especially in flowerbeds, as pure urine can burn the roots of some varieties.

The implications of a nationwide garden-potty are catastrophic. Although litres of water would be saved by not flushing, the damage caused to the environment by peeing in the open far outweighs any benefits. Once absorbed into the soil, the potential for urine content to spread to neighbouring gardens, farms and water supplies is extremely high. This increases the spread of infections and xenobiotic compounds such as prescribed or illegal drugs expelled in the urine. Not to mention the smell a neighbourhood would generate if all its gardens were soaked in wee.

For those who only have a front garden, or whose gardens are overlooked by others, the legal repercussions of exposing oneself in public would be severe. It is still an offence to urinate in public (unless you're pregnant, in which case you have the right to go in a policeman's hat), so anyone seen doing it, even under the guise of saving the environment, would face criminal charges. If you really want to make a difference, then store your urine in sealed containers and sell it on to medical research facilities, or criminals trying to fake drug-tests, and then use the money to plant a forest in your neighbourhood.

How would I go about dyeing the Mediterranean a different colour?

In the case of most large bodies of water the safest bet would be to use an organic dye that would not significantly affect the pH balance. Providing the dye base was sourced from a plant or creature that was native to the fountain, river or lake in question, it shouldn't cause any dramatic environmental problems, although it is unlikely that any dye would have a lasting visual effect due to the presence of neutralising chromophore microbes in the water. These are the bacteria which break down waste products, stranded flip flops and urine in the sea.

While the Mediterranean poses a few strategic and legal questions in this respect, it would actually be the easiest of the world's seas to dye a different colour. Due to the fact that 21 countries border the Mediterranean, it has an abnormally high concentration of methanol and cliatrine, which are illegally pumped from sewage works into the sea. This, combined with decades of booze cruises, beach defecation and projectile-vomiting bungee jumpers, has caused a significant reduction in the number of chromophore microbes in the water (which is why parts of the sea are quite cloudy) and has eradicated its natural defence mechanism against alien chemicals.

The most effective dye to use would be a reactive one with a strong fibre substrate, as this would not need an excessively high temperature to take effect, meaning you could sneak down to the seaside to carry out the deed in the early hours of the morning, before even the keenest sun worshippers have risen. Potential dyers can be safe in the knowledge that their actions will not have a hugely negative environmental impact on the sea, as it's already in quite a bad way. The few remaining fish that consider it home will not be affected, as years of human faeces and cheap beer in their bloodstreams have caused genetic colour-blindness. Perhaps purple would be nice?

If there was a storm in a teacup would the teacup break?

The last reported storm in a teacup took place in a small Devonshire kitchen in June 1992. Mrs Balcombe, a farmer's wife, had just put a sausage casserole into the oven for her husband's dinner when she sat down to drink a cup of Britain's favourite brew with a few digestive biscuits. Whilst dunking her second biscuit the cup began to shake and, before she had time to react, a tiny bolt of lightning zapped the biscuit from her grasp and whipped it into the cup, where a violent storm ensued. The tea pelted down on itself as gusts of wind thrashed it from side to side within its tiny china boundaries, amidst the sound of crashing thunder and lightning. The storm lasted for two days and by the end of the ordeal Mrs Balcombe vowed never to dunk a biscuit again.

Emergency response people who were called to the scene said if it hadn't been for her quick thinking, moving the tea cup outside and onto the front lawn, then the vibrations of the storm would certainly have caused the china cup to fall from the table and shatter on the kitchen floor. Unfortunately, she was unable to prevent a serious fracture on the inside rim of the cup. Beveragologists who examined it immediately afterwards blamed the storm on a combination of low air pressure, fresh milk (her husband was a dairy farmer) and the saturation levels of the dunked biscuit. They reported that the liquid movement to volume ratio was unlike anything they had seen previously, and if the storm had lasted another hour then the combined build-up of heat and friction would have undoubtedly blown the delicate bone china cup apart.

The Teacup Commission – a select committee set up to establish what future storm prevention measures should be taken – were careful to add that a teacup had never been broken in this way before, and that the public should continue to drink and dunk as usual.

The Wind-up Letters

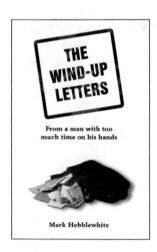

Mark Hebblewhite

£6.99 Pb

ISBN 13: 978-1-84024-534-9

From a man with too much time on his hands comes this collection of barmy correspondence, guaranteed to bring a smile to even the most poker-faced customer services assistant.

Whether he's appealing to the British Lubrication Federation for advice on resolving his cat flap predicament or making an enthusiastic request to Tiffany & Co for Tiffany's autograph, Mark Hebblewhite knows how to test professional patience. If you've ever wanted to ask McVitie's whether a custard cream is really just an albino bourbon, this book has the answer – as well as the answers to some other questions you might never have thought to enquire about.

Mark Hebblewhite has been a lifeguard, a waiter and an international personal banker, as well as a vegetarian butcher and a folder of cardboard boxes in a soap powder factory. He lives on the Isle of Man.